MASTERING *the Art of* Stress Management

A 30-DAY GUIDE TO
CLEARING THE MENTAL CLUTTER

Mastering the Art of Stress Management
A 30-Day Guide to Clearing the Mental Clutter

By **Sirshree** Tejparkhi

Tejgyan Global Foundation is a charitable organization
with its headquarters in Pune, India.

ISBN : 978-81-69572-31-6

Published by WOW Publishings Pvt. Ltd., India

First edition published in May 2026

Printed and bound by Trinity Academy For Corporate Training Ltd, Pune

This book is based on the Hindi book titled,
Let Go Tanaav by Sirshree Tejparkhi

To all those
who remain calm amid moments of turmoil
and continue to engage in their impersonal service.

Contents

SECTION III

Underlying Causes and Solutions for Stress

Preface

Row the Boat or Sail the Ship?

Imagine you want to travel to an island. You have two options to reach there: a boat or a ship. If you choose to travel by boat, you have to manage everything yourself. To move forward, you must row the boat until your muscles scream. You are responsible for carrying enough food and supplies. You are the navigator and the cook. You must guard the boat against the turbulent waters of the unpredictable sea and safeguard yourself from marine life. It is an arduous, solitary, and challenging journey.

On the other hand, if you travel by ship, you can take full advantage of every amenity on board. While you dine in the restaurant, relax by the swimming pool, and enjoy the vibrant company of fellow passengers, the ship's captain expertly navigates the route. A dedicated crew works tirelessly to ensure your safety and well-being. You are not battling the ocean; you are moving through it with grace.

Which option will you choose?

The choice seems obvious. No one would willingly choose the grueling labor of the rowboat when the sanctuary of the ship is available. Yet, when it comes to navigating our life's journey, many of us row the **boat of stress** rather than sail the **ship of understanding**.

If you row the boat of stress, worries and anxieties constantly bother you – whether in relationships, finances, health, or career. If you travel by the ship of understanding, you can navigate life's challenges with a sense of calm and clarity and attain your goal peacefully.

Then, why do we choose to row when we could sail?

The difference lies in our understanding and perspective on everyday events, whether we perceive them positively or negatively. Life is a relentless series of events – a succession of changes, challenges, and unexpected moments. Everyone perceives them through their own unique lens of understanding. Their deeply held beliefs and understanding greatly influence their response.

For instance, some people find climbing a mountain both exhilarating and relaxing, while others may find it intimidating. Similarly, driving is a fun pastime for some, but a stressful chore amid traffic for others. Even watching a match on TV is stressful for some, fearing their favorite team might lose, while others simply soak in the thrill of the game.

Thus, the same situation can be a source of pleasure for one and of agony for another, purely because of their differing understanding and perspectives.

If you perceive life through the lens of negativity, even a trivial mishap can feel like a storm. But if you view life positively with understanding, you can navigate even major incidents with a sense of calm resilience.

Pause for a moment and contemplate: In which situations do you feel stressed? How do you react when confronted by a new challenge? What is your perspective on looking at life? Can you approach life and its challenges with a fresh, positive, and correct understanding?

Most often, when stressed, people avoid confronting problems and turn to quick distractions, such as watching TV, using their mobile, shopping, or gaming. However, these are merely temporary remedies; you must seek a lasting solution to be stress-free.

While circumstances may change, if you develop coping mechanisms and inner strength to navigate life's challenges, you can easily sail through them and achieve your goal.

Human life is a divine creation, inherently designed for a stress-free, peaceful existence. It is time to abandon the boat of stress and board the ship of understanding.

This book is your invitation to board the ship of understanding. It is designed to offer you 30 tools to declutter, the right perspective, and the clarity needed to make your life's journey not just well-managed, but blessed and beautiful.

Let's make our journey blessed by mastering the art of stress management and embracing peace and relaxation.

How to Read the Book

We live in a world obsessed with external fixes. People often seek various therapies for their physical ailments, such as mud therapy, physiotherapy, ultrasonic therapy, Bach Flower therapy, and others. We have a remedy for almost every physical ailment under the sun.

But what happens when the ache is internal? What do you do when you are constantly under mental stress and unable to confide in others?

This book serves as a self-help resource. By embracing the techniques outlined in this book, you can effectively say goodbye to your stress.

The book is divided into 3 sections, each covering different types of techniques. However, you do not need to work on all techniques at once; instead, focus on practicing one technique each day.

SECTION I: The techniques in this section are simple and easy to implement. If you are feeling overwhelmed by stress and want quick relief, you can start by exploring any part of the first section.

SECTION II: This section covers techniques such as meditation and contemplation, which involve sitting quietly for a while in one place to reduce stress. When you have 10 to 15 minutes, practice these techniques for effective stress relief.

SECTION III: This section aligns with your ultimate life purpose, enabling you to embark on a spiritual journey.

SECTION I

Quick Fix to Alleviate Stress Instantly

1

Stress is Auspicious

Stress is a useful exercise for the mind and body if the mind is not stressed over it.

If someone told you, "Stress is auspicious," you might laugh it out. After all, you have likely spent years trying to escape it. In fact, just thinking about stress can be stressful for many. Considering it to be auspicious and a blessing may seem far-fetched. However, stress can indeed be auspicious. Let's understand it with some examples.

- Many students plan to study regularly throughout the year but fail to do so. When exams approach, they become stressed and rush to cover their entire year's syllabus in just one month. They even pass with good grades. How do they manage to study in one month that they could not do all year? Their intense stress becomes the driving force behind their studying, giving them the motivation they need.
- When employees face an endline for completing their work, increased work pressure makes them work faster and complete their tasks more quickly.

- When business professionals face the risk of potential business loss, that stress motivates them to devise new strategies to promote their businesses.
- If someone has to give a speech on stage for the first time, they naturally feel stressed. The stress makes them thoroughly rehearse speaking in front of a mirror before facing the audience. Consequently, they deliver an excellent performance. Once the speech is over, they feel relieved.

Thus, stress acts as a catalyst for a positive change. Stress is essentially a response to pressure from the surrounding environment, circumstances, relationships, and the workplace on the body and mind. It is a gift, a power, and a system provided by nature to cope with dangers and confront challenges effectively. After the event, stress naturally subsides.

However, stress is often perceived negatively. It is frequently misunderstood and deemed harmful because of its inappropriate proportion. A moderate amount of stress can be an invaluable asset for raising awareness and bolstering strength. Triggering necessary changes enables the body to adapt to situations. When stress arises at the right time and in the correct proportion, it leads to the desired outcome.

Consider a beginner who wants to exercise. If they push themselves too hard by lifting heavy weights, they overstrain their muscles and quit in pain. If they lift too little weight, their muscles wither from lack of challenge. But if they lift a moderate load, their muscles grow stronger.

Stress works exactly the same way. If someone thinks, "I should never feel stress," they are misunderstanding stress. A life with zero stress is a life of stagnation. Every living being experiences some form of stress at both physical and mental levels. It is a natural phenomenon of life.

In certain situations stress can actually enable us to perform new, larger tasks more effectively. For instance, a springboard in a swimming pool is placed under tension to enable powerful leaps and high jumps. If the springboard were to say, "Why am I being stretched and put under tension? I don't want this stress," you would realize its folly. For the springboard to perform its function, that kind of tension is necessary.

During the COVID-19 pandemic, everyone experienced significant stress, which made them more aware of their health. They started practicing Yoga, Pranayama, exercises, and mindful eating.

Stress is beneficial if it increases our awareness and boosts efficiency. However, it becomes counterproductive when it overwhelms the mind. Thereafter, the mind gets into incessant chatter, comparing, judging, and labeling everything as good or bad. It recalls similar memories of unpleasant, unsuccessful events, trapping us in a cycle of negativity.

It keeps complaining, "No, no, I can't do this work. It's impossible. I couldn't do it in the past and can't do it now." As the mind starts rambling, work begins to worsen; consequently, it poses roadblocks to progress. Then the mind justifies itself, saying, "See, I told you from the beginning; I am not capable of doing it."

It is important to recognize and address this mental stress to prevent it from affecting our mental ability and productivity. Let's understand this with an example.

> Sumit was preparing for his Medical entrance exam, facing stiff competition. He kick-started his preparation by creating a timetable. He diligently solved the practice questions daily provided by his teacher. As the subjects were tough, he experienced stress. To cope with this stress, he pushed himself to extend his study time from 5 hours to 10 hours a day. Consequently, his grasp of the subject deepened, enabling him to solve more questions in less time. This stress was natural, given his prayer to become a doctor. The stress served as a propelling force that honed his skills and bolstered his readiness, a challenge he embraced with a positive outlook.

A year later, an important exam was scheduled that would determine everyone's ranking in the state. Sumit prepared vigorously. However, his rank turned out to be very low, far below his expectations. He panicked and felt, "It is impossible for me to succeed." Overwhelmed by stress and anxiety, his focus drifted from his studies. His motivation to study began to wane. He started avoiding his classes. Whenever he tried to concentrate, his mind would grow restless and chatter, "The competition is too tough. There are more competent students than me. Getting admitted to a reputed college seems out of reach."

Sumit lost his self-belief and eventually gave up, thinking, "There's no way I'm getting selected this year." This negative mindset significantly impacted him. He began distancing himself from his study group and lied to his parents that he was studying with them. To seek temporary relief, he started hanging out with the wrong crowd and fell into wrong habits.

Initially a positive force, stress eventually turned negative, leading Sumit into a downward spiral of despair. He soon found himself trapped, sinking deeper into a terrifying grip of his own mental stress.

Always remember that stress precedes every success. All successful people, whether leaders, actors, business owners, or athletes, experience stress, but the difference lies in how they handle it. They do not stress their mind over stress. Even when their mind is stressed, they ignore it and focus on improving their work and moving forward.

Therefore, in the future, when you say, "There is so much stress," ask yourself, "Is this stress productive or counterproductive? How can I convert it into a blessing?" Have faith that if your mind is not stressed about stress, you can achieve anything. Nothing can stop you from succeeding, and most importantly, nothing can make you unhappy.

Action plan:

Identify situations when stress is productive or counter-productive.

2

Blow the Inner Whistle

When a cry for help arises from the depths of stress and sorrow, it transforms into a prayer. Such a prayer manifests conditions that allow one to live the life they desire.

When one is stressed, they want a simple yet powerful technique to release their stress instantly. Let's understand it with an example of a pressure cooker.

> A pressure cooker generates steam to cook food. When the steam pressure reaches its threshold, the whistle blows to release excess steam through its pressure outlet. Then, steam is generated again and escapes once more.
>
> Imagine if there were no whistle on the pressure cooker. What if the steam could not escape? Without a way for the steam to vent, the internal pressure would build until the force became strong enough to blow the lid off.

We also need an inner whistle to release our excess stress well before it reaches a breaking point and takes a toll on our physical and mental well-being. Once the excess stress is released at the right time and in the right way, the appropriate stress becomes a productive force.

It propels us to accomplish our work. Let's understand this with an example.

> When Harish started his new business, he struggled to gain momentum and felt stressed. However, rather than succumbing to it, he used it as a fuel. He channeled that energy into studying market trends and seeking innovative ways to attract customers. Consequently, his persistence paid off, and his business began to thrive.

However, when faced with adverse situations, many people become so overwhelmed by stress that they cannot think of ways to get out of them. Only when this excess pressure is released can they channel stress into a productive force that helps them reach the solution.

Mantra

One of the most effective ways to blow the whistle to relieve stress is through the repetition of a mantra. When you feel the pressure rising, repeat the mantra: "I am an integral aspect of God. No stress can harm me. With God's help, my stress is under control."

Trust that God is our ultimate caretaker. If He provides for creatures in the deepest oceans, He will certainly care for us. With this realization, this mantra will instill a newfound faith and confidence to face challenges. When this inner whistle starts blowing within you, the appropriate stress will become instrumental for your growth.

When stress begins to exceed its limit, remind yourself, "This stress is useful because nature wants to accomplish something through me." Silently affirm, "I am an integral aspect of God. No stress can harm me. God is my caretaker, and He is looking after me every moment."

When stress intensifies physical pain, first calm your mind by focusing on your breath, then repeat the mantra in your mind, "I am a child of God. God is my caretaker. So, no illness can touch me." As you find relief from stress, your body begins to support the healing process.

When you feel stressed at work or in your daily tasks, affirm, "I am a child of God. So, no stress can touch me."

Some people feel stressed by past traumas. If a past accident makes you anxious to drive today, remind yourself of the Law of Averages, which states that out of the many times you have driven, an accident occurred only once or twice. The likelihood of another accident is minimal. Fearing that it will happen again is futile. Then repeat the mantra, "I am a child of God. God Himself is protecting me. No stress can break my courage." This mantra will work like magic. The faith it awakens will calm your mind and help you move forward with your task.

Do not wait for a crisis to repeat the mantra. Repeat it during the mundane moments of daily life. With repetition, it will penetrate deep into your subconscious and become your core thought. Eventually, your mind will automatically blow the inner whistle the moment stress arises.

Prayer

When stress reaches its peak, a cry for liberation rises from the depths of the heart. It takes the form of a prayer, and through it, the path to freedom begins to reveal itself. As soon as we receive guidance from within, stress begins to fade. Many struggle simply because they are unaware of this invisible law.

A baby cries when hungry; that cry is its prayer, and the mother responds by feeding it. But was the milk created only after the baby cried? No, it was already available. Similarly, the solution to every problem already exists; sincere prayer helps bring the solution to light.

Prayer is the supreme power that can easily resolve any problem, from the trivial to the major, because it connects you directly to the Divine. The strength of prayer is truly immeasurable.

To harness the incredible power of prayer, learn to set aside your ego and pray with complete faith and surrender. Practice prayer even before stress arises, so that when the time comes, you can use it with complete faith in the right way.

During times of stress, offer the following prayer with deep devotion:

I am at peace in the presence of the Divine.
I am experiencing eternal peace.
I have been created by God,
hence, peace and bliss, which are the very nature of God,
are pervading my heart and mind.
God has created nothing to disrupt this peace.
Whatever the reason for my unrest,
it is not on that Supreme Power's list.
I surrender myself in the lap of God,
just as a tired child finds comfort in its mother's lap.
Waves of joy are rising within and all around me,
and I am feeling the presence of peace all around.
Peace... Peace... Peace...
O God, I am eternally grateful.

Action plan:

1. Identify situations where you can repeat different types of mantra.
2. Reflect on the power of prayer.

3

Recognize Stress as Something Insignificant

While shifting focus is important, what you shift to matters.

Rajesh was working in his office when his boss suddenly approached him and placed a file on his desk, saying, "Leave everything else and prepare this crucial report by lunchtime. The report should be on my desk in 2 hours."

Rajesh felt stressed. "How is it possible? This report takes at least 8 hours to complete. It's practically impossible to complete it in 2 hours." He began complaining about his boss, but immediately became aware that stress was building within him. He calmed himself and stepped away from his desk. After a short walk in nature and a few deep breaths of fresh air, he felt rejuvenated and returned to his desk. Then, he worked on the report at twice the normal pace and completed it on time.

You need to learn exactly what Rajesh did to relieve stress. Whenever you find yourself in situations where stress creeps in, recognize it first.

Then, work through it effectively to return to a balanced state. Let's understand these steps.

1. Become aware of the imbalance

Most people are blind to their own stress until it is too late. Often, those around them notice their irritability or erratic behavior first. By the time they realize what happened, they are left with a hazy memory and a heavy dose of regret, wondering, "Why did I react like that?"

While everyone experiences stress, some people are so sensitive to it that they can easily recognize its symptoms and immediately sense changes in their emotions. Once they become aware of it, they can take steps to reduce or eliminate it and move toward a balanced state.

Therefore, first, enhance your sensitivity to stress. Even if you notice a slight change in your behavior or find thoughts passing through your mind causing you stress, immediately recognize them. Whenever you start feeling irritated or shouting at those around you, or feel pressured by work or someone's remarks, immediately ask yourself, "Is this thought, event, or task causing me stress?"

When you become mindful of your stress, you are better prepared to manage it. With practice, you will gradually begin to identify stress in its infancy, so it does not escalate from the magnitude of an ant to that of an anaconda, and you regain your balance.

It is very important not to be careless with stress or push it beyond its limits; work on maintaining balance. With continued practice, you will come to know when stress arises in your body.

2. Change the topic or place

One of the most effective ways to relieve stress instantly is to change the topic, place, or activity. Thereafter, you will perform the task more effectively with renewed energy. It is a law of nature: when you change the topic, place, or activity that caused stress, your vibration shifts, allowing the stress to dissipate on its own.

These strategic breaks are not a waste of time. They are an investment in efficiency. Let's understand this with some examples.

- Many IT companies nowadays automatically lock computer screens after a few hours of work, forcing employees to step away and unwind. This prevents prolonged, uninterrupted screen time.
- Some people experience digital fatigue. As soon as they start working on their computers, they feel stressed for no apparent reason. To combat this, they can close their eyes for 5 to 10 minutes and listen to music, engage in light banter with colleagues, or watch a short comedy skit to feel relaxed. This small shift prevents burnout and improves efficiency and productivity.
- As board exams approach, students often experience significant stress. They become anxious, "What if I forget everything I have studied?" or "How will I revise such an extensive syllabus?" However, some students take short breaks during their studies and engage in hobbies or activities they enjoy. They might make a small painting or sketch, play a musical instrument, hum a song, or walk in nature. This helps them relax, avoid boredom, and memory freeze, allowing them to return to their studies with enthusiasm.
- During childhood, we all intuitively drew pictures of birds, butterflies, flowers, petals, etc., on the last page of our notebooks. This activity is known as doodling, a natural relaxation technique. When your mind is in turmoil, focusing on a simple creative act shifts your attention from stress to the beauty and abundance of nature. This shifts your vibration and allows the mind to relax. Even today, many therapists recommend this to relieve stress.

While shifting focus is important, what you shift to matters. Choose a topic or activity that promotes creativity, positive thinking, and increases your efficiency rather than hindering it. It should positively reinforce and bring out the best in you. Otherwise, in an attempt to change the topic, you may fail to take advantage of the constructive pressure needed to finish the task and lose sight of the significance of the work altogether.

Nowadays, many people try to escape stress by indiscriminately indulging in their smartphones. They spend hours watching short videos and scrolling through reels, unaware that they are trapped in the internet's maze and wasting their precious time. Thus, while attempting to avoid the adverse effects of stress, they end up jumping from the frying pan into the fire by misusing smartphones.

When faced with academic pressure, many students fall into the wrong company. While seeking relief from short-term distress, they inadvertently invite lifelong complications, such as bad habits or addictions. Therefore, intentionally cultivate healthy hobbies so that, when stress arises, you can devote time to them and regain the strength to work once you are stress-free.

Practice identifying stress in small events of your daily routine. As you become more sensitive to stress, you will become adept at recognizing it as it arises. Immediately change your place, topic, or activity. This will help you feel relaxed, replenish your energy, and return to work with renewed enthusiasm. Through daily practice, you will achieve mastery over this and become capable of handling even the larger storms of life with ease.

Action plan:

1. Identify the hobbies you want to cultivate to divert your attention from stress.
2. Reflect on the place, topic, or activity you will shift to when you are under stress.

4

Listen As if You Were Deaf

When you hear people criticizing
or speaking ill of others,
increase your ability to
"Listen as if you were deaf."

"Listen as if you were deaf" might sound like a paradox—how can one hear without listening? It does not mean physically covering your ears with your hands to block everything out or to shut the world. Instead, it is the art of selective listening: paying attention to the person while remaining unaffected by their words, especially those that disrupt your inner peace.

It is human nature to make a mountain out of a molehill—take a small, insignificant comment and blow it out of proportion. We struggle to handle negative remarks, cling to them, replay them in our mind until they spiral into significant emotional stress. Let's understand it with some examples.

1. Sheela went to party with her friends. Her friends chose to play a game where they had to share about each other's strengths and weaknesses. Everyone was enjoying the game until it was Sheela's turn. She took the remark to heart.

Her mind was overwhelmed with thoughts, "Am I really that bad? Do they really think this of me? Are they mocking me behind my back? Are they even my friends? Are they intentionally humiliating me?"

The emotional distress was so intense that she walked out of the party and later distanced herself completely. Though it was a lighthearted comment, her mind exaggerated it to the point that she began to believe it was true.

2. Rajni recently got married. When some of her mother-in-law's friends visited her home, her mother-in-law remarked, "Rajni didn't know how to cook before marriage, so I had to teach her everything. I have taught my own daughter everything so her mother-in-law wouldn't need to work as hard as I did."

   Rajni sensed sarcasm directed at her and got upset. The same thoughts kept repeating in her mind, and a sense of inferiority took root. To prove her worth and earn her mother-in-law's praise, she undertook all the household tasks alone. However, the resulting stress and physical exhaustion eventually took a toll on her health, and consequently, her efficiency deteriorated.

We often expect others to say what we want to hear, based on our expectations. When this does not happen, we become upset. Furthermore, we repeatedly repeat those words in our mind, fueling negative emotions and stress, even though the other person may have said them only once. To avoid such stress, listen as if you were deaf; ignore insignificant remarks to break free from this cycle.

If Sheela had kept the game spirit and disregarded the remark, she would have avoided stress and maintained her friendship. If Rajni had listened to such insignificant comments as if she were deaf, the comments would not have spiraled in her mind, causing her stress.

Many times, we allow minor issues to weigh us down at the cost of our happiness and allow stress to overpower us. Pause a moment to reflect on your current and past activities that caused you stress.

Sometimes, observing others' behavior triggers sorrowful thoughts within us. During such moments, disregard negative thoughts and channel them in a positive direction. Ignore things that lower your consciousness and drain your energy, and instead, learn from them and move forward.

When someone speaks negatively or criticizes you, do not feel sad or get angry at them. Instead, tell yourself, "Whatever they said reflects their perspective. I need not feel upset about it." Extract what is helpful from the conversation and ignore the rest. Instruct your mind to listen as if you were deaf. Even this single thought will work wonders in your life; you will neither take on stress nor pass it on to others.

Similarly, information or news from social media can become a source of stress. Therefore, listen to them with a firm resolve, "Whatever doesn't matter to me, I will listen to it as if I were deaf."

Ignoring is a powerful tool. It means consciously overlooking or not paying attention to something. Some people struggle to ignore what they hear on news channels, and those stories keep running in their minds. Their minds become overloaded with distressing images, which negatively affect their lives.

> Once, a couple was going on a picnic. The wife declared, "Today I will drive." The husband warned, "If you drive, we'll start the trip in the car, my dear, but end up as the headline for the world to hear."

People are often bombarded with so much news about accidents that they believe they are at risk of similar misfortunes. Therefore, those who tend to dwell on negative thoughts must harness the power of ignoring. They must cultivate the skill of selective listening, focusing on positive information while disregarding stress-inducing content.

Meditation on indifference

Let's practice a meditation on indifference to develop the ability to listen selectively and master the art of ignoring. Here, indifference means ignoring or neglecting, choosing not to give excessive importance to something. It is not about being careless but rather about making a conscious decision not to overprioritize something, even when fully aware of it. First, read the instructions and then practice them.

1. Sit in a comfortable posture with your spine erect.
2. Close your eyes and take a few deep breaths. Be detached from your body.
3. If you feel any sensation, discomfort, or emotion in your body, ignore it. Do not judge or label it as good or bad. Simply acknowledge that it is not for you, it does not concern you. It is to be ignored.
4. After doing this for a while, observe your thoughts with an attitude of ignoring them, as if they have no existence. Sit with the conviction that no thought can disrupt your peace. Remain in a state of indifference.
5. Training the mind to remain in this state of indifference leads you to a pause in reactions and brings a state of stillness. This brings the state of detachment.
6. Reflect on how detachment can help you in different aspects of life, and where a sense of indifference would be beneficial.
7. Imagine yourself practicing indifference toward your body and mind in various situations from morning to night.

After practicing this for a while, slowly open your eyes.

Practicing this meditation will help you observe or witness stress-triggering situations with indifference. With consistent practice, ignoring stress-inducing elements will naturally become your way of being.

Action plan:

Practice listening as if you were deaf in a situation and write your experience.

5

Don't Stress About Stress

The state of balance between emotion, action, and thinking is the ideal point.

The human body is so complex and full of wonders that even scientists have not fully understood it to this day. The most important part of the body is the brain, which governs every aspect of human life. Although it appears to be a small organ, it possesses an auto-system that enables the body to function smoothly and heal itself.

The body contains several glands that secrete hormones to maintain internal balance, homeostasis, even when slight imbalances occur. These hormones, unique to each gland, regulate our daily activities with incredible precision. The amygdala—a small, almond-shaped structure located deep within the brain's temporal lobes—coordinates with these glands. The amygdala works closely with the hypothalamus and plays a significant role in processing emotions and regulating responses to stress.

From childhood, whatever we have experienced or even seen in movies is etched into our brain as memories. These memories have shaped our beliefs about what is good or bad, how we judge behavior, when we should grieve, and when we must flee. When confronted with a similar situation, the amygdala springs into action and instinctively triggers the release of stress hormones.

It continuously monitors external situations, orchestrating and balancing emotions, actions, and thoughts to help us navigate threats or dangers. Understanding the appropriate balance of emotions, actions, and thoughts in any situation is essential. If the balance is appropriate, stress will quickly dissipate; otherwise, it will increase.

For instance, when a person is grappling with heartbreak or suffers a financial loss in their business, their emotions can spiral out of control. They become overwhelmed by emotions like grief, anger, fear, or anxiety. Their ability to reason and act decisively wanes. They struggle to find direction or act. Their emotions, actions, and thoughts are in overdrive. The surge in emotions creates a chemical imbalance in the brain, leaving them feeling even more helpless, hopeless, and unable to cope.

When a stressful situation arises, the brain immediately signals the release of chemicals based on past memories. However, if emotions, actions, and thoughts are not balanced, these chemicals stagnate in different parts of the body and eventually manifest as illnesses.

For instance, when stress is at 100%, emotions remain highly negative, accounting for 60-70% of our attention; thoughts become stagnant or directionless, accounting for only 15-20%. Actions are either nonexistent or minimal, limited to crying, shouting, or similar behaviors, contributing only 5-10%. This creates an imbalance in the emotion-action-thought ratio, with 70% emotion, 20% thought, and 10% action, highlighting how disharmony fuels stress. Hence, to truly overcome stress, balance emotion, action, and thought.

In ancient times, when humans lived in jungles, illnesses were less prevalent than they are now because, as soon as stress arose, they took immediate action. Their emotions, thoughts, and physical actions happened simultaneously. For instance, if they encountered a dangerous animal, they would instinctively flee to safety, and their thoughts would race to find a safe place. The adrenaline rush triggered by fear would prompt them to take immediate action. There was no time for the chemicals to stagnate in the body.

However, today's situation is different. Modern sedentary lifestyles often lack the physical activity needed to trigger this natural response. Therefore, whenever stress arises, consciously check whether your emotions, actions, and thoughts are out of balance—whether you are overwhelmed by emotions and not taking any action. Let's understand how to balance these chemicals.

Don't stress about stress

Consider the immense pressure shouldered by leaders, sports icons of the country, or corporate titans. The weight of their responsibilities is staggering, yet they carry it with quiet resilience. In contrast, our everyday stresses, often trivial by comparison, can feel overwhelming, as if pedaling a heavy bicycle up a steep hill. On the other hand, those at the pinnacle of success, like leaders of the nation, often remain composed. This is because they understand and embrace stress as an inevitable part of life, refusing to be consumed by it.

Ordinary people feel stressed from minor issues and also by the fact that they are stressed, resulting in double stress. Therefore, start by at least not letting your stress stress you out. When stress arises, accept it and tell yourself, "Wait, Watch with Wonder," also known as "WWW."

Just as we patiently wait for a website to load, similarly, we should wait patiently when stress arises, watch the situation unfold, and marvel at how things eventually resolve. Acceptance and patience are the keys. Life's challenges often hold hidden opportunities, and the act of waiting can reveal the path forward.

Identify stress trigger points

People often experience recurring stress in response to specific events, situations, or words. These are commonly known as stress trigger points. These triggers can vary from person to person because each one has a different level of sensitivity and a different way of reacting, shaped by their past memories. These triggers can spark feelings of tension, pressure, or nervousness.

For example, for some parents, their children's exams can be a stress trigger point. As exams approach, they become more stressed than their children. For some homemakers, "What should I cook today?" can be a stress trigger point. For others, "What should I wear to the party?" can be a trigger point. Traveling can be a stress trigger for some, while the weather can trigger stress for others.

There are many types of stress trigger points. If you identify them, you can prepare yourself to tackle them in advance. For instance, parents know that their children have exams every 3 to 4 months. If they monitor their children's daily study, instill consistent study habits, and provide regular support, they can remain stress-free during exam periods. Similarly, if a homemaker plans what to cook the next day on the previous night or creates a weekly meal plan, they can avoid daily stress. With a little preparation, they can manage potential stress effectively.

Just as a doctor carefully examines a patient to understand their illness, how long it has lasted, and its impact on the body before prescribing appropriate treatment and dietary changes, we need to first identify our stress trigger points so that we can take proper steps to address them.

Action plan:

1. Contemplate your stress trigger points and how you will address them.
2. Experiment with "Watch, Wait with Wonder" in a stressful situation.

6

Harness the Power of Words

Choose positive words to express or describe your feelings. This will positively influence your mood.

When faced with negative situations, we often describe our state internally, saying, "I am very scared," "I feel very insecure," "I am shocked," "I am anxious," "I am feeling bored," "I am tense," "I am angry," "I am sad," "I am feeling worried," "I feel restless," "I am depressed," etc. We tend to label our emotions negatively. However, by constantly repeating such negative sentences, we get trapped in our own words, become entangled in them, and assume they are reality. We rarely pause to question ourselves, "Is it really so? Do I need to feel so stressed?"

Therefore, whenever you try to articulate your emotions in words, be mindful to consciously choose positive words so you will feel that way. Otherwise, you will end up feeling negative.

No event is inherently stressful. The way you perceive it, the words you use to describe it, and the way you label the emotions that arise within you determine whether the event is stressful.

Often, people push themselves into suffering by labeling their emotions with the wrong words. They fail to realize that their own words become the cause of their sorrow. If you express your emotions in positive language, the negative ones will lose their power to hurt you.

Therefore, instead of saying, "I feel unsafe," try reframing it as "I feel the need to be cautious here." Likewise, rather than saying "I am stressed," consider saying "I am in a state that requires greater awareness." This simple shift in expression can transform your perception of the situation, foster resilience, and turn uncertainty into mindful action.

If you label your emotions as "stress", stress begins with that very word, and you feel your energy drained. For instance, if you are asked to think of an apple, a picture of a red apple will appear in your mind; hardly anyone would think of a green apple. Similarly, just thinking about your favourite food makes your mouth water. This experience is common to all.

This implies that the words we speak conjure images in our mind, and these mental pictures visibly affect our body. The mere act of thinking can trigger physical sensations. Having understood this, avoid using the word "stress"; instead, use a different word in its place.

For instance, instead of saying "The situation is stressful," say "This situation offers me an opportunity to remain calm" or "This situation is challenging." This positive reframing will shift your internal state from feeling overwhelmed to feeling empowered; you will experience a surge of energy, enabling you to take purposeful action.

Words like "challenge" and "opportunity" resonate with positive energy, naturally fostering courage and inner strength. By reframing your emotions with the right words, you can transform any situation into a challenge or an opportunity for growth and fully enjoy it.

Always remember that whenever negative emotions arise, they signal that something unusual is happening outside your daily routine. Do not get caught up in them by using negative words.

Whenever you feel stressed, reframe it by saying, "I am carefree," and feel that emotion for a moment. What image arises within you? You feel completely relaxed, and every cell in your body feels energized. Thus, consciously choose words that form positive pictures in your mind. When stress arises, rather than resorting to familiar negative expressions, cultivate the habit of using empowering language. Developing this rich habit may take time, but once ingrained, it becomes an integral part of your life.

If you are unable to find the right positive word to a feeling or situation, reassure yourself, "Right now, I am passing through a stress tunnel, which is going to end soon," or "Even in this stressful moment, I am able to remain peaceful." This paints a picture in your mind that stress is only temporary and is already on its way out. Soon, the situation will change; it is not permanent. Otherwise, stress can cloud your vision, leaving you feeling trapped and helpless. If this state persists for a long time, some people can even experience depression. However, by calling it a "stress tunnel," you affirm that it is bound to end because every tunnel eventually has an exit.

It is important to remember that negative emotions are transient and do not define our reality. Instead of dwelling on negative thoughts, use positive language to cultivate a more optimistic perspective.

If you truly wish to lead a stress-free life, resolve firmly: "No matter what happens, I will refrain from negative talk."

In stressful moments, instead of speaking loudly, speak in a soft, low tone to prevent stress from escalating. Take a firm vow, "I will not raise my voice or say anything hurtful to anyone, regardless of the situation." No matter how challenging the moment, even in the face of a great calamity, do not resort to abuse.

Otherwise, people vent their stress by lashing out at others. They use abusive or inappropriate language even in minor incidents. As a result, the other person, who could otherwise help, feels hurt and refrains from helping. This creates a hostile environment where cooperation stops and progress stalls, increasing stress levels. Then people say, "Misfortunes never come singly." But in reality, we breed new problems ourselves through uncontrolled speech and a lack of restraint. By losing our temper, we turn a single challenge into a vicious cycle of stress and further difficulty.

Therefore, you must also take this vow: "I will never speak words I would not be willing to sign my name to." If you cannot stand by your words, do not speak them. Do not speak under pressure, only to regret it later.

It can be challenging to recall these resolutions in the heat of a stressful moment. Therefore, cultivate the habit of choosing and speaking the right, positive words long before such a situation arises. With practice, you will naturally articulate your emotions and circumstances constructively, even under pressure, and avoid unnecessary conflicts to foster healthy relationships.

Action plan:

1. Reframe 2-3 negative sentences you say when you are stressed.
2. Experiment speaking softly when under stress.

Inner Magic
Refer to this book by Sirshree for deeper understanding

7

What is the Worst That Could Happen?

Do not get entangled in "What people will say."
To escape the stress caused by others, ask yourself,
"What's the worst that could happen?"
Then face your fears.

A major cause of stress is the fear of "What will people say?" Someone rightly said, "The greatest burden is living under the weight of others' opinions." On the surface, it may seem insignificant, but the burden of others' opinions can really cause stress.

In India, weddings transcend mere celebrations; they are powerful statements. Even families of modest means often go to extraordinary lengths, stretching their finances to ensure grand, flawless weddings, particularly for their daughters. The powerful desire to uphold tradition and impress in-laws, coupled with intense peer pressure, frequently overshadows financial prudence. Families often spend beyond their means to shield their daughters from future criticism, leading to significant financial strain and, in some cases, crippling debt.

People often suppress their deepest desires, burying them beneath the weight of societal expectations. Paralyzed by the relentless whisper of

"What will people say?" they silence the voice of their dreams. This constant suppression inevitably leads to stress.

> Roshan completed his engineering degree and settled into the steady rhythm of a conventional job. Yet part of him craved something more. He harbored a deep passion for tennis, not just to play it but to master it as a career. When he finally mustered the courage to share his ambition, his family's response was sharp and dismissive: "Have you lost your mind? After all the money we've spent on your education, do you want to waste it on tennis? How much will you earn? How will you survive? Think of your future and marriage!"
>
> Their words became an unwelcome echo, making Roshan apprehensive. He reluctantly shelved his interest, conforming to their expectations and pursuing a conventional path. Still, deep down, the question lingered: "What if?" Each time their discouraging words resurfaced, an inner conflict raged—the heavy burden of their opinions battling the persistent whisper of his dreams—fueling anxiety that gradually spiraled into stress.

The fear of "What will people say?" often prevents people from embracing new beginnings and acting on their inner aspirations. Consequently, they remain restless and dissatisfied. If you, too, are consumed by these thoughts, realize that people are bound to say this when they feel insecure about themselves and doubt whether you can accomplish it.

Do you also lack faith in yourself? Do you hold yourself back from new ventures because of others' opinions? If you trust yourself and your inner voice, isn't it high time to shed fear and stop seeking external validation? Contemplate, "Am I willing to truly choose to live my own journey, or will fear and the need for approval continue to steer my life?"

Those who are bold and carefree choose to dream and experiment, earning them an enduring place in history. Eventually, even their skeptics will concede, "We always knew there was something unique about this individual." While every leap into the unknown invites critics, the challenge is to live freely without letting their opinions define your choices. Do not let society define your goals or dictate your path to success, nor should you chase approval from others, as it will only lead you astray.

For instance, imagine a relative dismissively says, "You'll never achieve anything." That might ignite a fire within you, and you resolve to prove them wrong, fueled by the sting of being undervalued. Driven by this grudge, you work tirelessly until you finally park your new car right outside their house. But is buying that car your goal, or just a reaction to silence them? Do you really need the car, or are you simply chasing their validation?

To avoid these pitfalls, cultivate mindfulness. When criticized, focus on your breath to detach from worry and stay relaxed. It also reduces the unnecessary weight you give to external judgments, letting you focus on what truly matters.

Being bold and carefree is not about the adrenaline-fueled recklessness often portrayed in movies. It is a state of mindfulness and mental relaxation. It is not about comparing yourself to others or seeking to impress. Rather, it is about challenging yourself to improve daily and working with unwavering determination. Let's understand this with the example of the great mathematician Srinivasa Ramanujan.

> In his childhood, Ramanujan struggled academically in all subjects except his true passion, Mathematics. Time and again, his exam results showed failure in every subject except Mathematics, where he consistently excelled. Frustrated by his perceived limitations, his teachers dismissed him as a lost cause, declaring, "He will never achieve anything."
>
> Yet a pivotal moment arrived when a mentor observed Ramanujan developing innovative mathematical theories and instantly recognized his extraordinary talent—much like a jeweler unearthing a hidden gem. Despite his teachers'

persistent doubts, Ramanujan pursued his passion relentlessly, ultimately becoming a renowned mathematician. His story powerfully demonstrates the transformative power of self-belief. Today, his name is etched in history alongside Aryabhata's as a celebrated mathematician, a timeless reminder of the incredible impact of self-belief and perseverance.

Imagine a social gathering where someone accidentally stains their outfit. This seemingly minor incident can trigger a spiral of anxiety: "What will people think of me? My dignity is ruined!" In reality, no one cares. Most people are so preoccupied with hiding their own perceived flaws that they never notice others' flaws. Yet we continue to agonize over judgments that do not exist.

Therefore, remind yourself that everyone has flaws. The key to a stress-free mind lies in embracing imperfections. Stop letting trivial remarks or imagined judgments dictate your self-worth.

Being carefree and light-hearted is truly a state of mind. To achieve this, take a U-turn and venture into something new. Engage in activities that make your mind feel resistant and stressed.

As you step into the unknown, your mind will generate endless fears: "What if this happens? What if that?" To overcome this, tell yourself, "What's the absolute worst that could happen? I won't die and it's better to die than to live in such constant fear. It is safe to move ahead. Therefore, I am releasing all fears and inviting my future growth."

Remind yourself that past anxieties rarely became the catastrophes you feared. Stress distorts reality, magnifying problems that seldom actually happen. Therefore, these thoughts cannot be trusted.

If you are nervous before a job interview, ask yourself, "What's the worst that can happen? I simply won't get something I don't already have!" As you think this, your fears vanishes, and you naturally receive everything for which you are prepared, according to your originality.

Trust that the universe has a divine plan for each of us, and what is truly meant for you will manifest at the right time. Embrace double faith: "I may not get what I desire, but I will certainly receive what I deserve and am worthy of." This conviction allows you to approach challenges with trust and serenity and live a truly bold, carefree life.

Visualize that even if you don't get this job, something better is waiting for you. Every setback opens a door to better opportunities. When consumed by fear or anxiety, affirm, "What's the worst that could happen? God has given us the strength to face it." Thinking this way frees the mind from unnecessary worry and makes it carefree, aligning it with the effortless flow of life.

> Imagine a businessman who received a huge order and purchased all the raw materials to prepare for it. But for some reason, the order was canceled, causing him immense stress. The old way of thinking would be to panic and ask, "What will happen now?"
>
> However, with a new carefree mindset, he can ask, "What's the worst that could happen? Let's see what comes next." This simple shift in perspective can calm his mind, foster a sense of possibility, and allow innovative ideas to flow freely, transforming a perceived setback into a creative opportunity.

Just as tiny raindrops eventually form vast rivers, our persistent efforts, no matter how small, can bring about a great transformation in our life. So, let go of fears and anxieties; embrace a bold, carefree mindset to let your life unfold in its natural, free-flowing way.

Action plan:

1. Identify areas where you are afraid of "What will people say?" and do not explore new paths.
2. If someone comments or criticizes, practice mindfulness by focusing on your breath.
3. Practice asking yourself, "What's the worst that can happen?" when your mind is overwhelmed with fear in a new venture.

8

One Day at a Time!

Learn to organize all tasks effectively,
while being calm in the present moment.

Imagine stepping into a massive library, with three huge clocks—Whisper, Thunder, and Shimmer—hanging on the wall, each ticking in a steady, relentless rhythm. Whisper breathed a soft, rhythmic secret into the room. It was answered by the heavy, rolling strike of Thunder. But above them both hung Shimmer, whose ticking was not a sound but a vibration, marking time long before the library was built and long after the books turned to dust. Whisper ticked first, then Thunder, then Shimmer, as if they were engaged in a rhythmic trio in the language of their ticking.

Once, someone asked them, "How many times do you tick in a minute?" The clocks responded, "60." Then they were asked, "And what about in an hour?" They replied, "More than three thousand five hundred times." "What about in a day?" "Slightly more than 84,000 times." "How about in a year?' "More than 30 million." "Alright! And if your lifespan is 100 years, how many times would you tick in total?" Their answer echoed, "More than the world's population—more than eight billion times."

With the thought of ticking more than a million times a day, Thunder collapsed, and all its gears and springs fell apart. On the other hand, Whisper did not break; it continued to tick, with immense tension in its springs. Each tick was filled with strain and struggle. Meanwhile, Shimmer thought to himself, "I need to tick just once at a time, not all at once. No matter how many times I must tick for the rest of my life!" It continued to tick with calm and ease.

Pause and contemplate: How do you live your life? Do you mirror the calm resolve of steady Shimmer, the frantic pace of tumultuous Thunder, or the burdened humility of Whisper? Let's understand the depth of this analogy using some examples.

1. Rajat was a thriving entrepreneur. But suddenly, one day, his life took a devastating turn when his business venture with a close friend suffered a massive loss. The setback cost him everything—his land, property, and assets. Subsequently, he found himself consumed by relentless thoughts like, "What will happen now? What do I do? How do I manage my business and household responsibilities? How will I pay my children's school fees? What about their future? I have a younger sister to support. How will I fund her marriage? Why did I trust my friend so blindly? I feel like I've failed in life. It's all over. I'm powerless to do anything now." These concerns weighed heavily on his mind. Stress consumed him to the point that one day, he suffered a massive heart attack. His body could not withstand such unrelenting emotional and mental strain, and he died like the clock Thunder.

2. Nimisha grew accustomed to handling stress. It became an integral part of her routine. From the moment she woke up, an incessant chatter in her mind overwhelmed her with stress. "I need to finish my morning prayer rituals, prepare breakfast, then lunch, and do the laundry. Will the maid show

up? Will I finish everything on time? Oh, dear, I have to do all this work entirely by myself—so many responsibilities fall on my shoulders. I need to get the groceries from the market, too, and of course, ensure the children are enrolled in a good school so their future is secure. There's hardly any time for me. When will I get breathing space? Will my life always be a never-ending to-do list?" The constant mental strain began to take a toll on her health. Despite her ability to handle the workload, she remained stressed throughout the day. She lived life like Whisper, who was constantly under stress.

Most people are accustomed to living with the stress of future tasks. As a result, they cannot harness their full potential at work in the present moment. In the example of the clocks above, Shimmer had the wisdom that it had to tick only once at a time—meaning it focused on one task at a time. So, it could function effortlessly. If you also want to live like Shimmer, you have to chant a slogan to gain its understanding – "One Day at a Time."

Understand that you do not have to live your entire life in one go; rather, just as the clock ticks only once at a time, live only one day at a time and perform only one task at a time. "One Day at a Time" is the mantra. If you live life this way, you will live a spontaneous life like Shimmer. You will be free from the overwhelming burden of stress you carry. This does not mean you should not plan your activities. Do the planning, but do not take on the stress of the tasks.

Nature also demonstrates the principle of "One Day at a Time." A seed never worries about how large a tree it should become or how many flowers and fruits it should bear. There is neither competition nor stress. Everything unfolds in harmony according to the laws of nature.

"One Day at a Time" means just live for a day and see how your stress vanishes. Every year, life presents us with a great gift. If you open it, you will find small, unique treasures in the form of 365 days. Living each day in a new way is a gift in itself. Isn't that exciting? Yet very few realize this. So why not start living with this new understanding from today? Let's begin the day with this thought: "Today, events will unfold as they are meant to, but I will live one day at a time because my perspective has changed." Take the following steps to live like this.

1. **Create an F.D. of tasks:** Here, F.D. stands for Future Diary. Whatever tasks you want to perform in the future, whether tomorrow, the day after, or anytime later, write them in the F.D. It is often observed that while performing one task, our mind keeps reminding us of other tasks. For instance, "Tomorrow is the last date to pay the online taxes or bills; my car servicing is due; I must visit the tax consultant," and so on. Consequently, this never-ending to-do list keeps spinning in our mind, causing constant stress and leading us to believe there are too many things to do.

   However, if you simply write these tasks in a diary, you will be relieved of stress. You can then pick up tasks from the F.D. that need to be completed each day and work on them one by one. For the remaining tasks, tell yourself, "These are future tasks; I will see them in the future." Let's understand this with an example.

   > Kiran was the Chief Financial Officer of a large company. Along with managing the company's finances and a team of employees, he managed his family life and relatives. Despite the countless duties, he lived a surprisingly stress-free life only because of his habit of writing F.D. He wrote all the tasks for the upcoming month in it and tackled each day's tasks with peace and clarity. This habit allowed him to effortlessly accomplish many tasks each day with greater energy, without being burdened by stress.

   You might wonder, "Is it really that simple?" Well, it is not easy, but it is not difficult either. You have already written tasks for today with their designated times. Now, follow the mantra – "One Day at a Time" – and complete them one by one. Tasks for tomorrow will be addressed tomorrow, and so on. This is the significance of living with "One Day at a Time."

2. **Bother then, when then becomes now:** This is the mantra for living in the present. When future anxieties creep in,

immediately repeat this mantra to break the chain of thoughts. Tell yourself, "I will worry about the future when it comes. I stay in the present for now and harness the moment." With this understanding, you will learn the art of living in the present. Let's understand this with an example.

> Asha's son was studying in college, but she was always overwhelmed by worries about his future. "What kind of job will he get? How much will he earn? What about his marriage and the family? How will my daughter-in-law be? We'll need to build a new room for them," and so on. In these moments of anxiety, if only Asha recalled the simple mantra, "Bother then, when then becomes now," she could be relieved of the anxiety and stress about the future.

It has been observed that whenever people think about the future, they tend to focus more on the negative. On the contrary, if they adopt the mindset of "Bother then, when then becomes now" and learn to live in the present, new, creative solutions begin to emerge.

Our heart beats only once in a moment. Our breath follows a natural rhythm of inhalation and exhalation. There is neither impatience nor haste to complete the task; everything unfolds in its own time. Nature's ways are simple yet effective. Therefore, take both steps and live a life free from stress, move through each day with grace and ease.

Action plan:

1. In which situations will you practice "One Day at a Time?"
2. In which situations will you practice "Bother then, when then becomes now" mantra?
3. Create a Future Diary of your tasks.

What to do when the mind troubles you
Refer to this book by Sirshree for deeper understanding

9

Conscious Self-Reporting

Negative self-reporting is a major cause of stress.
Therefore, at the very least,
ensure you report to yourself the right way.

Modern life has become so mechanical that we have lost the art of prioritizing time for ourself amid the daily whirlwind, leaving us constantly stressed. As we grow exhausted from facing sorrows and struggles, our inner voice, once a guide, has fallen silent because we have stopped listening to it. As a result, it is only natural that negative thoughts increasingly dominate our mind, deepening our pain.

However, if we can turn these negative thoughts into positive ones through conscious self-reporting, we can feel happy amid the same circumstances that were causing us stress and sorrow. Let's understand this with an example.

> An announcement was made on a flight that its takeoff would be delayed by several hours due to a technical glitch. Aboard were two passengers—Aarav and Nirav—both en route to crucial work meetings. After hearing the announcement, Aarav instantly became anxious, consumed by thoughts of

> disrupted work, incomplete tasks, and potential loss. Nirav, though initially concerned, quickly accepted the situation. Settling back, calm and composed, he reassured himself, "Whatever happens, happens for the best." He could say this because he changed his self-reporting.

Whenever an incident occurs, our mind immediately reports on it: "This is good," "This is bad," "It should have been like this," "It should not have been like that," "This is right," "That is wrong," "This is unfair," and so on. Such self-reporting by the mind and the emotions it triggers causes us distress and tension. Therefore, even if you cannot change the external circumstances, you can change your self-reporting about them and keep stress at bay.

Whenever the mind says, "I am sad," consider reframing it, "I am allowing myself to be sad." This prompts a powerful question: "If I can choose to allow sadness, who is stopping me from being happy? I can also allow myself to be happy." This implies that the power to experience joy or sorrow lies inherently within us, not in external happenings.

Self-reporting can be passive or active. Passive reporting tends to magnify negative thoughts, leading to undue stress. Active reporting, in contrast, helps quiet the mind by releasing thoughts that cause tension. Active reporting aims to soothe a troubled mind and cultivate a sense of detachment from external circumstances. No matter what happens in the outside world, stay mindful of how you report it to yourself and always keep your self-reporting active. Let's understand this with an example.

> Three farmers—Rohan, Sohan, and Mohan—were working in a field. Rohan was unhappy, Sohan was busy and indifferent—neither happy nor sad, while Mohan glowed with health and happiness. When asked, "What are you doing?" Rohan replied, "I am toiling to make my living." Sohan said, "I am working to provide foodgrains for others." Mohan proclaimed, "I am working in harmony with the nature created by God." His self-reporting was that he was

performing divine work. Therefore, he could happily endure any hardships.

Externally, all of them toiled hard in the scorching heat and lifted heavy loads; they faced the same situation. Yet Mohan remained healthy because of his self-reporting. He could see his toil as a joyful collaboration with divine creation, transmuting the drudgery into a celebration and easing his burden.

Pause and contemplate: Do you want to become unhappy, troubled, and stressed by external events, or do you want to change your internal reporting to live a healthy life?

You are a traveler on the journey of life. Your body is the boat that carries you. How do you want to sail it? Do you sail it, treating it as a burdensome duty, a misery, or a forced obligation? Or do you sail it, considering it divine work, with the spirit of love and devotion? Just as a boatman joyfully helps others reach the shore, you can make yourself happy and healthy and become instrumental for others.

Let's understand how you can turn stressful situations into opportunities with a story.

A saint once visited a potter's workshop and noticed a clay pot set aside from the others. Upon inquiry, he learned that the pot had a small hole at the bottom. The potter, frustrated, considered it useless and unworthy and discarded it. However, the saint asked him for this very pot.

The potter hesitated, saying, "Why do you want to buy this faulty one? Instead, buy a good one." But the saint kept insisting. Finally, the potter unwillingly sold the defective pot for a very meager sum. The saint took the pot, filled it with water, and hung it above an altar in a sacred shrine. The hole allowed the water to drip slowly and steadily onto the altar below—a perfect, continuous offering. The very pot that had caused the potter stress became a sacred instrument of devotion owing to the saint's wisdom.

Therefore, whenever you feel stressed, pause and examine how your mind reports it, what you are doing, and why. By consciously redefining the purpose behind the event, you can change its meaning entirely. This shift transforms the journey of life into a more enjoyable experience. The very thoughts that seem to be drilling holes into your peace and increasing your stress can be elevated to a higher, more meaningful purpose simply by altering a few key words in your self-reporting.

Let's explore how we can nurture the right kind of active self–reporting through some examples.

1. Passive reporting: "I am bored."

   Active reporting: "I am allowing myself to be bored."

   As soon as you say this, you will realize that if you can allow yourself to be bored, you can also allow yourself to become instrumental to a higher purpose.

2. Passive reporting: "This person is wrong."

   Active reporting: "They are not wrong; they are just different, driven by their own habits."

   This perspective will dissolve the complaint, easing the stress.

3. Passive reporting: "I am useless."

   Active reporting: "I am part of the Divine."

   This perspective shifts from temporary self-criticism to the eternal truth, restoring self-worth.

4. Passive reporting: "This world is a battlefield."

   Active reporting: "God is with me."

   With this shift, you move from a state of conflict to one of companionship and protection.

5. Passive reporting: "I always receive fewer comforts."

   Active reporting: "Nature has abundant resources, and they come to me easily and effortlessly."

With this shift, you move from a scarcity mindset to an abundance mindset, filled with contentment and gratitude.

6. Passive reporting: "I am sick."

   Active reporting: "I am allowing myself to be sick. If I can allow myself to be sick, I can also allow myself to be perfectly healthy."

   This shift gives the power to heal.

Transform every event and situation into a stepping-stone or an opportunity. View it as a challenge and learn to change your internal reporting. As you change your reporting, your stress will reduce. If you understand this secret and apply it in your life, the journey of your life can be more joyful and fulfilling.

Action plan:

Consciously change your self-reporting in situations where you feel unhappy and stressed.

10

Laugh at Your Stress

Laughter is a cure for every ailment of the body and mind. Only the wise know how to laugh at their follies.

The body and the mind are deeply interconnected, each profoundly influencing the other. Physical strain clouds the mind with despair, while mental strain drains the body of its strength and vitality. Recognizing this powerful link, psychologists devised a principle for controlling the mind by controlling the body. According to this principle, if we demonstrate patience and courage in our actions during stressful times, our mind will soon feel relieved.

The benefits of this practice extend beyond mere stress relief. It can also help cultivate happiness, self-confidence, courage, and overall well-being. Let us understand this with an example.

> Whether you are stepping onto a stage, into a party, or into an interview, if you feel fear, self-doubt, or a sense of inferiority, act as if you are being presented with an award for an exceptional performance. Walk as if you feel no stress. This immediate shift in mindset will transform your posture,

allowing you to stand tall, keep your chin up, and walk with poise. This physical shift instills confidence, making you feel fearless and relaxed. You will be amazed at how the simple act of acting confident can unlock your inner strength and free you from stress.

Until now, people have made the mistake of thinking, "I will walk tall and confidently only when I feel confident," or "When I am not stressed, I will be happy and smile." However, the psychological principle says, "Our feelings change according to our physical actions." Having understood this, do not wait for stress and fear to disappear; instead, proactively act with confidence and courage. This action will infuse you with new strength. Similarly, instead of waiting to be stress-free, practice being relaxed and confident in your daily life, while sitting, standing, walking, working, speaking, and listening for a few minutes every day. Through this practice, you will learn and master the art of managing stress in no time.

For instance, when you are sitting, take a moment to assess your posture. If you find yourself slouching, sit straight as if you are ready to face any challenge that comes your way. Open your arms and feel the joy of confidence and the lightness of being stress-free. Continue observing yourself as you walk, speak, and work. Whenever you sense stress, fear, or confinement, remember this powerful psychological principle: change your physical gestures to match those of a strong, confident, and courageous person. Act as if you are the offspring of a King, carefree and content.

People often struggle to begin new tasks because they mistakenly believe motivation must precede action. They wait for the "drive" to strike before starting, creating a psychological barrier. But what is the reality? Does action follow feeling, or does feeling follow action?

The reality is that action and emotion work in tandem; they go hand in hand. While a change in feeling can change your actions, a change in action can also change your feelings. By controlling your physical actions, you can regulate your feelings. In other words, by approaching a seemingly uninteresting task with enthusiasm, even if it is feigned at first, you will soon develop interest in it.

It is easier to act because our actions are more directly within our control, whereas our emotions and interests are not. With this understanding, do not wait for the right feeling or interest to arise; simply begin the work. Whatever work you do, act as if you are genuinely interested in it. Use your full willpower to do it. By understanding and applying this principle, you will become a true *Karmayogi*, living forever free from physical stress and mental burden.

Laugh at your stress

It is easy to laugh when life is going well, when your mind is at ease, and when stress is nowhere in sight. Even a fool can find joy in pleasant circumstances. There is nothing remarkable about that. But when things are not going your way and you are overwhelmed by stress, yet you are smiling—that requires true courage or an understanding of the psychological principle mentioned above.

It is not a big deal if you are laughing heartily with a perfectly intact and beautiful set of teeth. However, laughing out loud with broken front teeth takes courage.

In moments of difficulty, hopelessness, and stress, deliberately act out to laugh so that the stress begins to diminish. A gloomy face only amplifies your stress, and increased stress leads to more gloom, creating a vicious cycle of stress and sorrow. Break this cycle with the powerful antidote of laughter.

Laughter acts as a healing balm for every ailment of the body and mind. You feel lighter and more at ease. Yet very few truly know how to laugh at their own troubles, even amid overwhelming stress. Let's understand this with an example.

> Ram and Sham were studying together. While Ram was writing, Sham felt thirsty. As he drank, he accidentally spilled water onto Ram's book. The book got wet. Sham worried

about how Ram would react. In that moment of stress, Ram chose humor over anger. He said, "It's good that you don't drink ink!" Sham was taken aback and asked, "What do you mean?" Ram replied, "It's just water; it will dry. If you were drinking ink, my book would be ruined forever." Both burst out laughing.

You can see how laughter lightened the mood for both Ram and Sham. No tension arose between them, and the situation did not feel like a problem. Otherwise, there could have been arguments.

Henceforth, resolve to laugh when stress creeps in. If you cannot genuinely laugh, at least pretend to laugh at the stress. Only the wise truly know how to laugh at their own follies. Laughing at your own mistakes acts as a healing balm. When stress arises, laugh at your stressful state. If you cannot laugh, at least try to smile. This small act can turn your smile into genuine laughter. With that laughter, the problem appears insignificant, the solution becomes instantly visible, and the stress of that problem simply fades away.

The world moves with those who laugh, and it supports them. To solve a problem, cooperation from the world is crucial. The toughest problems can be solved easily and in less time with everyone's support. By working with a smile, problems are resolved quickly and effectively.

Do not wait for a reason to laugh. Learn to act happy for no reason. With a little practice, laughter will be your constant companion. Say goodbye to stress with a laugh!

Action plan:

1. Practice "Act as if" in situations where you feel stressed.

2. Laugh at your stress in some stressful situations.

11

The Non-Doership Mantra

When overwhelmed by a storm of stress, tell yourself,
"I haven't done anything till today,
and I don't have to do anything hereafter."

If you were asked to list all the pending activities you wish to complete, you would likely come up with a long list. Along with that list, a subtle yet undeniable pressure about how and when these tasks would be completed would also arise.

Put the book down and try experimenting with it.

Now, there is some good news! You do not actually have to perform any of the tasks you wrote. Yes, you read it right! You do not have to do them. In fact, the truth is that while you believe you have performed all the activities so far, you have not; they were actually performed *through* you. Hard to believe?

Think back to the time when you were an infant in a cradle. Were you managing your life then? Did you ever worry about getting milk, clothes, or toys? Not at all! Back then, you simply lay in the cradle, gazing at your toys, and everything was taken care of automatically for you.

Just as you were looked after then, you are being looked after even now. The only difference is that you no longer acknowledge this fact. This is because, until a child is around two or two and a half years old, they do not have a sense of a separate "I" or ego that takes credit for actions or believes itself separate from others. However, as they grow, people begin to tell them, "You did this. You did a great job. You'll grow up to be someone great. You will be that." This conditioning leads them to firmly believe that they are their body and that all actions performed by their body are their own. However, the thoughts and ideas guiding those actions are being *given* not only to their body but to all bodies.

The universal power that governs the entire universe also guides your body by seeding thoughts within you. You cannot generate a single thought on your own. However, once a thought arises within you, you can weave thousands of other derived thoughts around it. Yet the original thought is given to you; you do not generate it yourself.

Thoughts are given to you, and actions are performed through you, but later the separate sense of "I"—the ego—creeps in and claims credit for the actions. The reality is that you have never truly done anything until now; you are doing nothing at the moment, and you will not need to do anything in the future. All actions are happening automatically and spontaneously on autopilot, and they will continue to do so. Everything unfolds of its own accord.

As an experiment, set the book aside for the next 10 minutes, just sit back and do nothing, and observe what happens.

During this experiment, you probably noticed yourself doing small, unplanned things like glancing around the room, scratching your head, or changing your posture. Did you consciously decide to do any of these, or did they just happen? You will be surprised to learn that you did not think about doing any of them; they just happened. Everything is happening automatically and spontaneously, including your breathing. You do not consciously decide to breathe; it happens naturally on its own.

Now, if your actions are being performed by giving thoughts to your body, do you need to carry any stress about those tasks? So far, whatever your needs have been, the actions required to fulfill them have been carried out *by* you. Similarly, whatever your future needs may be, the necessary actions will be carried out by thoughts *given* to you. In other words, there is absolutely no need to carry the burden of tasks or responsibilities. By holding on to this understanding, you can live a stress-free life, not just from tomorrow, but from this very moment.

But what can you do about the mind that is conditioned to carry burdens every day? True to its nature, the mind will inevitably present you with a long list of tasks that will cause you stress. Thoughts like "I have to do this today," "I have to meet this person," "I must avoid meeting that person," and so on will keep surfacing.

So, what can you do to dissolve all these burdens at once and still get things done from dawn to dusk? There is a way to do it. You need to remind yourself of the non-doership mantra every day: **"I have not done anything till today, and I don't need to do anything hereafter."** The mantra helps you view every event from a new perspective.

You might wonder, "How is that possible? I did so much work yesterday, I am working today, and I have even more to do tomorrow." But as you just read, each of us is given some powerful thoughts, and actions happen automatically. Hence, you need to embrace the new understanding that the body operates like a machine, carrying out its tasks effortlessly. The body will do everything from dawn to dusk, and it should do so because it stays healthy only when it remains in action. The moment you drop the attachment to "I am the doer," you will experience a profound sense of peace and tranquility. This way of thinking is an act of Self-grace—a blessing you should embrace. It is as if Nature itself has taken responsibility for all your tasks, and your body is surrendered to carrying them out.

You can attain such a wonderful state, but initially the mind will resist with its logical reasoning, saying, "If I don't do anything, how will the work get done? Will my body just sit idle?" However, the mantra does not mean you should do nothing or that your body must be forced to sit idle. The understanding is that even with a non-doer attitude, much will happen automatically through the body.

For example, if you declare, "Today, I am not going to do anything," you will still notice that your body cannot just sit quietly. In a short while, it will get up, drink water, grab something to eat if it is hungry, take a walk, turn on the TV, chat with someone nearby, etc. In other words, actions will happen whether you intend them or not. The essence of the mantra is not to stop the body's activities, but to let go of the sense of doership and simply watch whatever happens as a witness without identifying with it.

In other words, there is nothing like "doing something," nor is there "not doing something." It is about observing how things happen without being the doer.

When there is ignorance, the sense of "I did this" creates resistance. You carry the mental burden, thinking, "I have accomplished these tasks, and I am yet to complete so many more." When the mind anticipates tasks for the next day, it triggers changes in the brain that release chemicals of fear, anxiety, stress, or excitement. However, through deep reflection and understanding, if you surrender to the truth that everything is happening automatically and spontaneously, you can say, "Today, I have not done anything at all. Everything is unfolding naturally, according to the divine will, for my well–being and growth."

Every day, your body will perform its tasks, yet you can remain free. Imagine the sheer bliss of watching it all unfold! As a detached witness, you simply observe how things unfold, and in that observation, your bliss remains undisturbed. The inner bliss of liberation that you are already free inspires the body to work with greater ease and happiness. Abandon the belief that you will be free only after retirement. Instead, consistently tell yourself and firmly believe that you are already liberated. Let this truth take root within you and awaken a new sense of purpose.

To anchor this mantra, repeat it again and again. If you forget it, remind yourself. If forgetting becomes a habit, write it down in a notebook or a diary: **"I have not done anything till today, and I don't need to do anything hereafter."** Read it regularly to reinforce it. This practice will help the mantra take root and become second nature.

Once you are clear that you never did anything in the past, you are not doing anything now, and you will not need to do anything in the future, you will experience complete relaxation. In this relaxed state of mind, you can achieve feats that others might struggle to accomplish together. Relaxation does not just ease the process; it elevates the quality of your work. Relaxation is an art that everyone should learn. Once you are relaxed, you become like a magnet, effortlessly attracting everything you need. Everything unfolds naturally, yet you are not doing anything. When life offers such an experience, it is only wise to make the most of it.

Action plan:

Sit for 10 min without doing anything and observe what happens.

SECTION II

Let Go of Stress

12

Releasing Theory

Release your worries and stress,
trust that the best solution will emerge.
This belief will open the path to stress relief.

You must have noticed that when rainwater stagnates in one place, mosquitoes and other germs begin to breed. Similarly, heaped garbage creates a foul stench. In that moment, the immediate instinct is to clear a path for the water to flow or to remove the trash and clean the area, knowing that leaving things as they are could spread disease. This primal fear of illness compels swift, decisive action, urging the cleansing of the surroundings.

However, what about the mental filth that accumulates because of the trash of negative thoughts? Are you aware of it?

Just as physical spaces collect clutter, our mind, too, gathers negative thoughts, and over time, they can fester and manifest as physical illness in our body. Yet no one reminds us how to clean this mental clutter, or even whether it needs cleaning at all. Neither do people instinctively practice inner cleansing.

Nature, by design, embodies a remarkable self-cleansing system for its elements. For instance, trees and plants are tireless purifiers, absorbing carbon dioxide and releasing oxygen. Oceans, with rhythmic precision, cleanse themselves by casting out impurities and pollutants with the low tide and drawing them back with the high tide. With every rain shower, nature washes away the accumulated dust and dirt from trees and plants, leaving everything wonderfully renewed and vibrantly alive once more.

Just as nature purifies the external world, it has also equipped us with an internal cleansing mechanism. With each breath, we effortlessly draw in pure air and expel impurities. Similarly, our body efficiently eliminates waste from food and water through its integrated excretory systems. These are all seamlessly automated internal functions.

Unlike our body's natural processes, our thoughts lack an intrinsic auto-release system. While nature persistently offers cues to help us shed our mental clutter, we often miss them. When we cling to negative thoughts, these critical cues emerge as unsettling emotions, physical discomfort, or various experiences, urging us to unburden ourselves, as if telling us, "It's time to release. It's time to let go." Unfortunately, if these reminders go unheeded, these suppressed emotions force their way out through anger, fear, agitation, and anxiety. Let's understand it with an example.

> Umesh was engulfed by a looming work deadline and mounting pressure from his superiors, feeling the intense grip of stress. This tension overflowed, leading him to lash out at his colleague, Mahesh. "Don't you understand something so simple? Don't you know what needs to be done and when it needs to be completed? Go and redo it, and make sure it is on my desk first thing tomorrow!" Unknowingly, Umesh had transferred his work stress onto Mahesh.
>
> Carrying this burden, Mahesh arrived home. His children greeted him eagerly, "Daddy, we want ice cream." His wife added, "Shall we have dinner early? Then we can take the kids out." But Mahesh, overwhelmed by the stress from Umesh's

> demands, unloaded it on his family. He snapped, "Someone's just back from work, exhausted, and none of you care! All you care about is going out and eating ice cream. You are all just lounging at home. You have no idea how stressful it is for me at work!"
>
> In this unhealthy chain reaction, Umesh's stress was passed to Mahesh, and Mahesh's inability to process it led him to offload it onto his family, highlighting a damaging pattern.

Eventually, we all release emotions, but often in ways that cause more harm than good. While some release them by talking, many release them through anger, which is often not the right approach. Releasing, however, is a beautiful gift by nature, but only when we practice it in the right way.

The relentless pace of modern life has fueled a surge in mental health challenges, such as stress, anxiety, and depression. Consequently, many are seeking support from psychologists or counselors. These professionals offer a safe space for people to freely unburden their minds and express their thoughts and emotions, often through insightful questions like, "What is bothering you? How does that make you feel? Is this event making you sad, angry, hateful, or resentful?" Their goal is to help clients delve deeper into their experiences, enabling them to process and release their emotions. They employ various therapeutic techniques to alleviate psychological discomfort.

Just as breathing is a natural process, it becomes *Pranayama* the moment you bring awareness to it. When you consciously focus on its rhythm—how long to inhale, hold, and exhale—it becomes an art and a technique that offers significant health benefits. In the same way, while releasing emotions happens naturally, if you learn some techniques for emotional release, they can profoundly improve your well-being.

In the forthcoming chapters, we will learn some stress-releasing techniques. However, before we delve into their details, it is important to understand exactly what happens with these techniques and what you need to let go of. Let's understand this with the help of two principles of the releasing theory.

Releasing theory: Principle 1

When we release negative emotions, we often experience a surprising ripple effect: many smaller, less obvious negative emotions are also released along with them, significantly lowering our overall stress levels.

When we release powerful negative emotions like anger, resentment, envy, or hatred, they often bring their "siblings," an entire "family" of related negative thoughts and feelings, with them. It is crucial to recognize that, beyond these strong emotions, our mind also clings to emotions like guilt, fear, and shame, as well as to deeply rooted beliefs like "People around me aren't good," "No one values me," or "No one loves me."

Various life experiences unknowingly leave emotional imprints that the mind holds onto, fostering deep-seated stress. This burden subsequently manifests as physical health problems, strained relationships, and stalled financial progress.

Releasing these thoughts and emotions dissipates all negativity. Despite this profound benefit, many people remain so identified with their emotions that they embrace them as an inseparable part of their lives and resign themselves to suffering as their inevitable destiny. This is unnecessary. As long as we hold on to these negative patterns, we will continue to face obstacles in life and remain adrift in a sea of stress. Thus, actively releasing negative thoughts and emotions is important for navigating life's challenges and cultivating a sense of peace and freedom.

Releasing theory: Principle 2

The second principle offers a counterintuitive insight: even attachments typically seen as positive can become a subtle source of stress. This includes dedication to a goal, the pursuit of harmony or attachment in relationships, or adherence to desires and needs. While it is certainly beneficial to have goals in life or to continuously work to harmonize relationships or please others, if these pursuits become a source of stress, they should also be released.

This principle also suggests that when you let go of your clinging to positive desires and aspirations without stressing over their outcomes, they often manifest in your life with greater ease and spontaneity. For instance, you set a goal but let go of your insistence on its fulfillment, adopting an attitude of "If it happens, fine; if it doesn't, no problem." When you cultivate a state of mind in which the outcome of the desire no longer disturbs you or causes you stress, you will observe that these desires begin to manifest in your life miraculously.

Now that you have gained this understanding of how to release stress, say goodbye to your worries and tensions and step into a happier, more fulfilling life. In the subsequent chapters, we will explore some techniques to help you release stress.

Action plan:

1. Write down the negative emotions that are causing you stress.
2. Write down your desires.

Emotional Freedom Through Spiritual Wisdom
Refer to this book by Sirshree for deeper understanding

13

The Art of Turning a Rock into a Rocket

Learn to transform your stress into a ladder or a rocket. View your stress with the right perspective and channel it to achieve miraculous results.

Tinku was in the tenth grade. His neighbor asked him, "What's the matter, son? I haven't seen you outside lately. You don't even go out to play anymore. Is everything alright?" "I am overwhelmed, Aunty!" Tinku confessed. "Exams are looming next month, followed by the pressure of admissions. But the real struggle is choosing a path. One person suggests engineering, another medicine, and others marketing or media. With so many voices and conflicting advice, I feel completely lost. I have no idea what I want to do in my life. This constant pressure is maddening, and frankly, I have lost all motivation."

In today's world, stress touches us all, shadowing children and adults alike. We are aware of its grip yet unable to release it, like a driver with a foot stuck on the brake. This constant tension makes life an uphill battle. Yet despite this awareness, we are unable to lift our foot off the brake, i.e., we are not releasing the stress. Learning to let go of stress is essential; otherwise, our journey through life becomes unnecessarily challenging.

Whether the stress is trivial or significant, we must become aware of it and acknowledge, "I am stressed right now." Otherwise, if suppressed, it becomes hard and immovable like a rock. When we are stressed, we feel heavy; when the stress ends, we feel lighter. We need to melt this rock in time and make it lighter, so it transforms into a rocket that soars into the sky and vanishes, leaving us light and free.

The following are a few steps that can help turn the rock of stress into a rocket to be released:

1. Being aware and understanding the level of stress

To uproot stress from its core, it is crucial to understand its intensity. The simplest way to do this is to notice whenever you feel even a slight shift in your feelings or when you find yourself getting irritated about something. Recognize that you are under stress. Gauge that stress on a level of 1 to 5, where level 1 is mild stress and level 5 indicates extreme stress. Let us understand them in detail.

- **Level 1:** This is a very minor form of everyday stress, often stemming from small, seemingly insignificant incidents. For example, the disappointment you feel if someone does not smile at you when they see you, or if someone does not offer you a seat, or does not talk to you.
- **Level 2:** This is a mild stress, slightly higher than level 1. For instance, the irritation you feel when you need to go out, but your car doesn't start, or breaks down in the middle of a journey, or runs out of fuel.
- **Level 3:** This is a moderate level of stress that begins to manifest physically. For example, the anxiety you feel when a family member falls ill, or the worry that sets in when your child is late from a picnic and you cannot reach them or their friends. The inability to contact them directly intensifies the stress.

- **Level 4:** The stress is so intense that it causes mental disturbance. For instance, the panic you feel if a family member meets with an accident or is diagnosed with a serious medical condition. Other triggers might include exam failure, the upheaval of relocating to a new city or country, an abrupt job loss, a business setback, or an unpredictable future.
- **Level 5:** This is extreme, unbearable stress that can persist for years. It can be triggered by a deeply traumatic incident, the death of a loved one, or a significant financial setback.

Using the 1 to 5 scale, you can assess your own mental state to identify your stress level. It is not necessary for everyone to experience the same level of stress in the same event. Stress levels can vary from person to person. The above examples are intended solely for understanding.

2. Accept the stress

Being aware is the first step to dealing with stress. Right after an incident, when the mind begins its endless chatter, we feel stressed. In such moments, fully feel the stressful thoughts, emotions, and their sensations in the body. Assess their intensity and ask yourself, "Can I allow this level of stress to stay with me?" If the answer is "Yes," that is fine. If the answer is "No," then ask, "Can I allow this stress to stay for a little while?" Often, the answer is "Yes." If not, try asking again after some time; you will likely find some level of acceptance. If you are still unable to accept the stress, repeat the question, "Can I let this stress remain for a little while?" By asking this question two to three times, the mind suddenly accepts the stress, and the stress level begins to drop.

Otherwise, as soon as the mind feels stressed, it instinctively seeks escape, often resorting to outbursts, irritability, or indulging in vices. Ironically, these reactions only make things worse, leading to more stress. However, when you allow it to remain even for a while, it loosens its grip. Now, you become its master by allowing it to stay.

3. Let go

Once you accept and allow the stress to simply be, it begins to loosen its grip, transforming from a rock into a rocket. Now, this rocket needs a spark to launch. Much like a Diwali rocket waiting for a spark to soar into the sky, your stress-rocket is primed for flight; it just needs ignition. The next question you ask yourself serves as that spark: "Can I let go of this stress?" The answer is almost always "Yes" because you understand the importance of releasing stress and living a stress-free life. However, it is crucial to say "Yes" loudly. People often ask the question but forget to affirm it with a resounding "Yes." Remember, saying "Yes" is crucial. By saying "Yes," you reclaim your power to let go. It is like igniting the rocket, launching it into the universe, and letting go of its hold on you.

4. The window of the present—The magic of "Now"

In this step, visualize a window opening in the sky. Your rocket soars toward it, ready to ascend into the vast universe. This window represents the present moment—the magic of now. Can you now let go of your stress-rocket to pass through this window? This window is your opportunity to release your stress and anxiety and embrace a state of relaxation. As you say, "let go," bring this feeling into your mind. "All the emotions, fears, anxieties, and restlessness rising from stress are leaving me; passing through the window of the present and disappearing into the vastness of the universe. All negative thoughts are also leaving me." Release all the negativity. All your stress has been released through the window.

5. Winergy—Win-Win energy

As the rocket of your stress passes through the window of the present, a second window instantly opens beside it. Through this window, a divine white light, i.e., winergy, showers down on you. As your rocket exits the first window, winergy descends upon you through the adjacent window. Embrace this feeling, knowing you have released all negative thoughts. You are now enveloped in positive divine light.

Winergy is positive energy—win-win energy. Just as energy is power or vigor, winergy is a positive, uplifting energy with benevolent intentions that we direct toward ourselves. Basically, we bless ourselves, wish for our own well-being, and give ourselves positive thoughts. We often direct positive thoughts and blessings toward others, but winergy is about blessing ourselves. Only when we are brimming with the winning energy of love and joy can we truly offer those same prayers for the well-being of others. Whenever you give yourself winergy, radiate divine light on yourself by affirming some of the positive sentences below.

- "I always dwell in the source of love."
- "I wholeheartedly spread good vibes and positive energy, ensuring all my actions are filled with goodwill."
- "I am good; I am truthful; I am part of the divine."

Let's understand how to use these five steps with an example.

> Vikram scored very well in tenth grade. However, as he was interested in graphic design and animation, he chose the arts stream. His close friend, Arun, chose the science stream. Later, Vikram completed his postgraduate studies and secured a job at a firm. Arun completed his postgraduate studies in Artificial Intelligence and secured a high-profile job at a Fortune 500 company.
>
> As a graphic designer, Vikram spent hours on social media for work. He also intermittently scrolled through the profiles of his former classmates. One day, while scrolling through Arun's profile, he saw that Arun was traveling the world, getting promoted at work, and buying a new house. Even though Vikram earned a decent living, he felt like a failure. Every time he saw a "success post" from Arun, he felt a knot in his stomach. He stopped scrolling through online profiles and even stopped hanging out with his friends because he felt inferior to them. He began to withdraw, lost interest in his job, and grew irritated.
>
> When Vikram was told the importance of letting go of stress to live a stress-free life, he was initially reluctant but eventually

agreed to try. Using the releasing technique, he followed the five steps:

1. **Being aware of and understanding the level of stress**

   He first noticed stress in his body. He found that feeling a knot in his stomach, feeling aloof, and feeling irritable were signs of stress.

2. **Accept the stress**

   He assessed his stress level and asked himself, "Can I allow this feeling of inadequacy to stay for a while?" At first, he wanted to run away from the feeling, so he immediately said, "No." But when he asked again, he let the stress linger for just a little while, and it eased slightly.

3. **Let go**

   He asked himself, "Can I let go of this stress?" and said "Yes" aloud because he wanted to live a stress-free life.

4. **The window of the present—The magic of "Now"**

   His stress was released through the window of the present, allowing the divine energy, winergy, to flow in through the adjacent window.

5. **Winergy—Win-Win energy**

   He prayed for blessings and repeated positive affirmations.

   - "I am happy and content with my talent."
   - "I am happy to contribute to the world in my own way."
   - "My creativity is a gift to the world, regardless of my bank balance."
   - "I celebrate others' success because there is enough room for everyone to perform and succeed."

He practiced this technique daily. Slowly, the grip of stress loosened, and he became completely stress-free. His relationships with those around him blossomed.

Similarly, you, too, must let go of the burdens of the past and the present workload, the taunts you receive from others, and the distressing thoughts about your health. First, relax by allowing these feelings to stay, and then release them by letting go. Then observe how the journey of life becomes smoother once you take your foot off the brake. Every time you "let go," you set yourself free from constraints and feel lighter.

Action plan:

Identify a stressful feeling you want to let go. Follow the 5 steps to turn a rock of stress into a rocket.

14

When in Stress, GIFT Yourself

Instead of dwelling on past events and feeling stressed, it is better to release them and enjoy the present moment.

There are many incidents in life that the mind clings to, refusing to let go. Whenever those memories resurface, it is as if the same old movie starts playing before our eyes. Although we might often believe that stress has trapped us, the reality is that we invite it by constantly dwelling on the past. By hoarding old memories, we repeatedly watch scenes from the past, relive those same emotions, and endure the same pain and suffering, thus inflicting stress upon ourselves.

Throughout the day, these past events keep running like programs in our subconscious mind in a loop. They are like modern-day animated GIFs, Graphics Interchange Format, used to convey messages. The moment we open that message, the graphical animation plays continuously until we close it. Similarly, these negative thoughts and emotions keep playing before our eyes, whether consciously or unconsciously, draining our energy and fueling stress. Now, stop these internal "GIFs" not by force but by releasing them using a specific technique.

When the GIF is combined with the right Technique, it becomes a GIFT. Whenever you feel stressed, use these techniques to release your emotions, negative thoughts, and feelings. The resulting joy and lightness you experience is a gift you give yourself.

Paper technique 1

At some point in your childhood, you would have made and flown a paper airplane. Do the same today, but use it as a release technique. Whenever you feel stressed, identify the underlying mental pattern triggering it. Whatever negative thoughts, complaints, anger, or guilt are swirling through your mind, write them down on a piece of paper. Some people even experience suicidal thoughts; write them down as well. Write down the mental patterns and the associated beliefs.

> For instance, if you are stressed about a lack of money, you might think, "No matter how hard I work, I never seem to have enough money, or even if I do, it does not last. There is never enough," etc. Take a moment to think deeply about whether, despite wanting to have more money, you secretly harbor beliefs such as: "Having wealth would be difficult to manage," "There is just too much legal paperwork involved," "There are a lot of taxes and taxation-related work," "Too much burden of maintaining accounts." With these beliefs, you might be unconsciously resisting the flow of money to avoid these perceived hassles. You may not even realize that your subconscious mind has been holding on to these limiting beliefs about money, due to which money never seems to stay with you.

All these programmed thoughts continue to play out as vivid scenes or pictures within you. Now, release these mental imprints and loosen their grip on your mind. Start by writing them down on paper and then folding them into a paper airplane. Find a place, maybe the terrace of your building or a hilltop, and let it fly away. You can even send it off into the air like a kite. In that moment of release, feel that all your negative beliefs, patterns, and assumptions that were causing distress have flown away, released into the vastness of the universe, and that you are now receiving *winergy* in the form of a gift.

For example, if someone thinks, "I am just an ordinary person. No one cares about me. Why do I always get picked on? I am helpless. I am tired of being the scapegoat at my workplace." It is as if a GIF has been turned on and is now playing in a continuous loop. Now, you need to release this loop and transform it into a gift.

Paper technique 2

In this technique, write down all your thoughts and limiting beliefs on paper. Then burn the paper as a symbolic act of letting go.

> Manish was struggling to find a suitable marriage partner. When he was told he was responsible for his predicament, he was taken aback. "That can't be true," he retorted. "I've signed up on multiple matrimonial sites and registered with every marriage bureau."
>
> However, when he was asked to reflect on his thoughts and beliefs about marriage, he discovered a deep well of fears. His persistent internal monologue was, "Marriage means more responsibilities. I can't take on someone else's responsibility. I can't handle someone's tantrums. How will I keep her happy?" and so on. These internal narratives constantly dominated his mind, strengthening his repulsion to marriage.
>
> To break free from this programming, Manish needs to confront and analyze his beliefs, gain a deeper understanding of relationships, and rewrite the negative internal script that kept him from moving forward. He needs to write down all his thoughts on a piece of paper and then burn it. While doing so, he should actively feel that all his negative conditioning and beliefs that are obstructing his marital aspirations are

being completely released. With this, all his limiting beliefs and perceptions will burn to ashes, and he will soon receive the gift of marriage.

Throughout the day, the mind is occupied with one topic or another. A moment ago, it was on one topic, and a moment later, it will latch onto something else, like a restless child running helter-skelter, picking one thing or another. But now you are equipped with techniques to stop it! You can release stress using any of these techniques. And don't forget to give yourself the gift.

Action plan:

1. Identify your negative thoughts that run as GIFs in circle. Release them using Paper technique one. Feel winergy as a gift.
2. Write down all your negative thoughts and beliefs. Release them using Paper technique two. Don't forget to give yourself the gift of winergy.

15

Releasing Meditation

Bring forth those tasks to which your desires or cravings are associated. Let them go through the Releasing meditation to alleviate stress.

Ashok had been living abroad for many years. Suddenly, for some reason, he was told he would need to return to India after 2 to 3 months. Having lived abroad for many years, he had accumulated a lot of belongings. He began worrying about what to do. Obviously, it was impossible to bring everything back—only a fraction of his life could fit on a plane. The sheer volume of things to manage was overwhelming.

A wave of perplexity washed over Ashok as he faced the decision of what to leave behind and what to take. He began mentally delegating his possessions, thinking, "This cupboard can go to this friend, and that table to another." This sorting was bittersweet. Parting with years of belongings brought a quiet sadness born of attachment to each item. Yet he felt consoled knowing they would be used by others. He decided to use the time he had wisely, first sorting through the items he felt clear about and setting aside others until he was more certain about their disposal.

Ashok's dilemma serves as a powerful reminder to let go of things you no longer need and are unnecessarily carrying that are causing you stress. These could be physical, mental, or emotional clutter that causes unnecessary stress. With the practice of the Releasing meditation, mindfully let go of what no longer serves you. For the things you are still unsure about, clarity on what to do will come to you over time.

Releasing meditation

In this meditation, you will focus on the cravings and desires of each of your senses and their functioning. For example, the function of the ears is to simply listen, so focus on listening to the sounds that arise. The function of skin is related to touch, so focus on feeling every texture and sensation. The function of the tongue is related to taste and speech, so focus on the full spectrum of tastes like bitter, sour, sweet, and spicy, or even the honey of sweet words or the sting of harsh words. Read the instructions fully before practicing the meditation.

1. Sit in a comfortable meditative posture and close your eyes.
2. Take three deep breaths. Inhale and exhale slowly to calm your mind.
3. Ask yourself, "What desires is my mind holding onto? Which desires have risen to a point where it is time to let them go? Is it right to let them go? Can I allow myself to let go of every thought, emotion, and tension, and be free from them?"
4. Pay close attention to the answer that arises after asking this question. The answer could be: "Yes, I can allow myself to let go of everything. I can let go of all that I have been holding onto."

5. As you meditate, have this understanding: when you become ready to let go of everything, that which is truly meant for you will return in greater abundance, and that which is not meant for you will dissolve. With this clarity, do not hesitate to release, for you have nothing to lose and the entire universe is there to gain.
6. Convince your mind to let go of everything, because only then will you fully benefit from this meditation and your life will be transformed.
7. Now, move to the next step and ask yourself, "What do I not want to see?" You may get different answers. For example, you might not want to see a certain color, dirt, or a child crying. Perhaps you dislike seeing someone else win an award. Bring every such desire to the surface.
8. Now ask yourself, "Can I really let go of these desires? Can I allow people to live their lives their own way and achieve their success?" The answer will be, "Yes, I can allow it; I can let go of this desire."
9. After a while, tell yourself, "Let go of this desire." As you say this, clench your fist and then slowly open it while saying, "Let go, let go." Mentally repeat, "I have now released this desire; I am free from it." After freeing yourself from this desire, move on to the next.
10. Pause in that stillness for a while. Then ask yourself, "What is it that I do not want to hear?" Various answers may emerge, such as unpleasant sounds, hearing others criticize you, chaos, the sound of barking dogs, and so on. Try to bring forth even the subtlest desires of your mind.
11. When all desires surface, ask yourself, "Can I let go of these desires?" The answer may be, "Yes, I can let them go; I can live a life free from these desires." With this response, clench your fist and slowly open it while saying, "Let go, let go." In this way, you are symbolically releasing all your desires.

12. Next, ask yourself, "Which tastes do I want to avoid, and which do I yearn to have always?" You will get different answers, such as bitter, sour, bland, spicy, sweet, etc. Now, turn inward and ask yourself, "Can I let go of my desire for all these tastes? Because what is meant for me will come back to me." Let go of all such desires for tastes that your mind is holding onto, no matter how much you yearn for them. Clench your fist and open it while saying, "Let go, let go." After opening your fist, say, "I have released all the desires for tastes."
13. By letting go of all sounds, sights, and tastes, the illnesses your mind has been holding onto will also be released. When one has to hear, see, smell, taste, or touch something undesirable and resists it, a blockage is created. These blockages cause diseases in the body.
14. During this meditation, let go of everything. Sometimes we hesitate to let go of something dear to us, fearing it will not return. Do not hold onto this fear, because what is truly yours will come back to you. Free yourself from every desire that creates a blockage. Once you are free from all such desires, feel the free flow of energy throughout your body.
15. Now ask yourself, "Which smells do I dislike?" Some people dislike the smell of kerosene, while others are troubled by vehicle exhaust fumes. Others may dislike the smell of smoke or a foul odor. Conversely, some people like certain aromas, such as perfume, scents, or soap fragrance. Recall all the smells around you.
16. Now ask yourself, "Can I let go of all these smells too?" The answer will be, "Yes, I can let them go and live a free life." With this response, clench your fist and slowly open it while saying, "Let go, let go."
17. When you are done, declare to yourself that you are completely free, then slowly open your eyes.

If you do not want to work on all the senses at once, you can focus on one sense per day. For example, you can start with the ears on day one, the tongue on day two, the eyes on day three, and on the fourth day, turn your attention to your thoughts, desires, and cravings.

Do not worry that letting go of your desires might cause you to lose your good traits. Always believe that what is truly yours will come back to you, and it will return even more abundantly. The visible and invisible blockages in your mind prevent you from realizing your highest potential. With this inner resistance, desires become an affliction, hindering your ability to work freely.

However, if you release these desires, all your good wishes will return to you, multiplied. You have nothing to lose and everything to gain. By practicing this meditation regularly and methodically, you can truly liberate yourself from the grip of desires and begin living a more liberated and fulfilling life.

Action plan:

1. Practice releasing meditation for all senses.
2. For next one week, practice releasing meditation for each of your senses - ear, eyes, tongue, skin, and nose. Then practice it for thoughts, desires, and cravings.

You are Meditation
Refer to this book by Sirshree for deeper understanding

16

Inflate the Balloon and Release

You can transform your sorrowful past
into a fun-filled episode
right now, in this very moment,
saving yourself from pain and despair.

Imagine you have a fever. You want to check your temperature to see how high it is so you can take medication and recover on time. If the temperature does not show up, you will never know whether there is a viral infection. You would say, "It's a good thing this fever warned me early to start treatment. It's good to know this." Similarly, when you feel anxious, stressed, or fearful, regard them as a useful indication to release and empty yourself from within, rather than suppressing or expressing them.

Let's explore another stress-releasing technique that is simple and easy to follow. You can use it when you are under tremendous stress and overwhelmed by a storm of thoughts. Even if you need to repeat it two to three times, you can do so to completely escape the whirlwind of stress. As you bring those thoughts into your awareness, you begin to break free from the grip of negativity. This allows you to watch your thoughts from a distance as a detached witness and release them.

It is a visualization technique that uses an imaginary balloon to release stress and emotional pain. Through this simple visualization, you will learn to lift the weight of your worries and watch them float away, reclaiming your inner space.

1. Visualize a balloon of any kind. It could be a colorful water balloon, a lighter-than-air helium balloon, or a simple one you inflate yourself.

2. Reflect on the different kinds of stress you are currently experiencing.

3. Now, assess the intensity of that stress. Then accept it and tell yourself, "Okay, I have this stress. Let it be. Let it stay for a little while. I allow it to stay in my body for a while, if it wishes to." Gently tap into those feelings and thoughts of stress with love. The more love they receive, the more they begin to dissolve.

4. Now it is time to release them. Visualize a transparent balloon in front of your eyes. Bring the balloon to the part of your body where you feel the stress. Visualize yourself transferring all your stress, anxiety, and sorrow into the balloon.

   Imagine the balloon inflating with a black, blue, green, or mud colored substance. As you transfer all your accumulated stress, pain, and worries into the balloon, tie a firm knot.

5. Now, release this balloon from your hand. Watch it float and drift away into space, gradually dissolving into the vast expanse of the universe and becoming invisible. Your anxiety, sorrow, and stress are dissolving into the universe. Feel that they have been released from within you.

6. Now observe yourself and feel whether your sorrow, anxiety, stress, and pain have decreased or completely disappeared.

7. If you still feel sadness and anxiety in your body, bring another balloon and fill it too. This time, you will notice that

this balloon is slightly smaller than the first. Tie a knot and release it into the universe as well.

8. Repeat the same procedure with the third balloon. Again, fill this balloon with your sorrows and let it dissolve into the universe.
9. Continue this practice until all your stress, negative emotions, and worries dissolve. Then, gently open your eyes and remain in this state for a few moments.

You might have seen a pressure cooker at work—how the whistle lifts to release steam once the pressure builds. When the whistle does not blow on its own, you manually lift it to release the pressure. In the same way, take charge and cultivate the habit of releasing stress on your own so you can live a stress–free life.

Action plan:

Practice the meditation given in this chapter to relieve your stress.

17

Emptying Meditation

Practice Emptying meditation to relieve stress.
Being still in meditation means "doing nothing,"
and "doing nothing" means letting go of what is unnecessary.

When weeds grow alongside crops in fields, they can damage the harvest. Therefore, farmers remain vigilant and remove them on priority. Once the weeds are cleared, the crop's quality significantly improves. Through this vigilance, the farmer receives full support from nature to produce a high-quality harvest. It is a beautiful gift from nature, rewarding the farmer's vigilance in caring for the crop.

Similarly, we too have cultivated internal weeds of various beliefs, tendencies, and notions within ourselves. They pose obstacles in our path, creating resistance within us, leading to increased stress levels.

Let's explore a technique to uproot these weeds and invite happiness and abundance into our life. By adopting this technique, you can remove these obstacles and release your stress. As you release the stress, you experience a sense of lightness, which is your true original nature. Thereafter, new ideas start emerging from within you, your hidden talents begin to surface, and your existing qualities get refined even further. All of these are bonuses and surprise gifts from nature for you. Let's delve into this technique and clear our path to embrace these treasures.

Whenever you are overwhelmed by stress, anxiety, or hopelessness, and the underlying causes of stress become apparent, visualize yourself becoming empty from within. Clench your fist and then open it, affirming "Empty it... Empty it..."

Emptying meditation

This is a unique meditation that you can practice alongside a devotional song.

1. First, read the meditation instructions and the lyrics of the Empty meditation devotional song given below. You can either record the song for future practice or memorize it for a deeper connection.
2. Now, as you listen to it, close your eyes, and hum along softly. While you do so, recall any negative thoughts, beliefs, and misunderstandings.
3. When you hear the words "Empty it," clench your fist. While saying, "Empty it," open your fist and lower your hands in a gesture of surrender. Feel these deep-seated burdens being released from your subconscious, freeing you from the underlying pain.
4. When you are guided to fill yourself with positive emotions, love, joy, and peace, draw your hands together to your heart. Feel the positive energy filling within you.
5. In this meditation, we will let go of what no longer serves us and invite fresh, positive energy and new positive qualities to enter us.

The Empty Meditation song

Empty it… Empty it… Empty it!
Empty it… Empty it… Empty it!

Let the prison of old beliefs now fall
And in that space, let peace stand tall
Empty the mind of all beliefs
Let go of the need for mere relief

Empty it… Empty it… Empty it!
Empty it… Empty it… Empty it!

Empty my eyes of sights that captivate
Fill them only with scenes that elevate
May my eyes not in glamor go adrift
May my gaze be divine and uplift

Empty it… Empty it… Empty it!
Empty it… Empty it… Empty it!

Empty the sounds my ears crave
So that I hear only what God says
May hymns of devotion grace my ears
May I revel in the divine silence I hear

Empty it… Empty it… Empty it!
Empty it… Empty it… Empty it!

Empty my tongue of delicious tastes
Free it of those tastes that it hates
Empty it of harsh speech that hurts
Fill it only with speech that comforts

Empty it... Empty it... Empty it!
Empty it... Empty it... Empty it!
Empty my mind of wishful thinking
Free it of tendencies overpowering
Grace my mind with the highest wisdom
So that I revel in supreme freedom

Empty it... Empty it... Empty it!
Empty it... Empty it... Empty it!

In this way, by practicing the above meditation along with chanting the devotional song, you can release your negative emotions and break free from the grip of stress.

You may have noticed that stress often resurfaces because we have suppressed it deep within. It is like some unused fireworks from a celebration are stored for later use and never used. They keep resurfacing, looming over the mind like a heavy burden. Hence, release them from within so that they are eliminated forever.

Action plan:

Practice Emptying Meditation.

18

Pause the Event and Decorate It

Revisit old negative memories in a playful way.
When you view those events in a new light,
the painful emotions associated with them begin to fade.

You may have heard, "Bury the hatchet and focus on the future," "The past is dead, focus on the future." People advise others to forget their past and focus on the present and future. They argue that old memories are worthless and only bring pain. But can we truly erase the past and find peace in the present?

The harder one tries to forget the past, the more it haunts them, more persistently than before. While trivial things fade with time, some experiences leave an indelible mark on the mind and heart, so deep that they refuse to fade. Despite the strong desire to let them go, these memories refuse to loosen their grip. For instance, things said to us as children can sink so deeply that they grow more vivid as we get older, rather than blurring with time. Back then, we did not have the wisdom to speak up for ourselves, and so we quietly accepted narratives of the mind. But over time, those very impressions begin to shape our lives, our perspectives, emotions, and choices. When a similar situation occurs, it triggers the original trauma, reopening the wound and causing even more intense distress than before.

Sometimes, long-buried memories resurface, leaving one feeling inferior, weak, or regretful about one's inaction. "If only I had spoken up then." They regret the past silence, endlessly rehearsing how they should have handled the situation. This triggers an endless, agonizing loop in which they mentally rewrite the script—rehearsing exactly what they should have done or said if given a second chance: "If that happened again, I'd do this, or I'd say that."

Childhood scars, such as being bullied in school, often refuse to fade. The mere memory of it triggers a wave of anger and stress. "Why couldn't I do anything then?" Many carry a lifetime of such emotional baggage. When a past trauma is triggered, the stress returns as if it is happening all over again.

Researchers studying human behavior have observed a recurring pattern. When certain memories resurface, they trigger the same surge of emotions felt during the original event. People instinctively resist these emotions. They try to chase them away at the earliest. But the harder they try, the more they actually end up amplifying them, proving the fundamental truth of the mind: whatever you resist, persists.

> Nitin, a 26-year-old, grew up in an authoritarian household. He watched his father exert total control over his mother's life. It was always his father's way or the highway: "Cook this," "Don't go there," "Don't talk to them." He witnessed endless arguments and, at times, saw his father resort to physical abuse. Now, his subconscious held a deep-seated belief that marriage is synonymous with pain and constant arguments between couples.
>
> As Nitin grew older, his family began discussing his marriage. However, he found himself spiraling into anxiety instead of feeling the expected excitement. He began suffering from an inexplicable ailment. He started having dizzy spells

and stomach cramps for no reason. Despite seeing several specialists and undergoing numerous medical tests, the results were always clear. The culprit was not physical but emotional. He was trapped in the shadow of his childhood, fearing that his own married life would mirror the toxicity of his parents. No one could pinpoint that a joyous occasion like marriage could paradoxically trigger deep-seated trauma. This was a classic case of past trauma sabotaging a present joy, a connection that remained invisible to everyone.

Nitin decided to seek help from a counselor. Over the course of several sessions, Nitin was astonished to discover that unpleasant, unresolved memories from the past were the root cause of his current distress and physical symptoms. Through these sessions, Nitin was introduced to specific techniques to dissolve the emotional weight of his past so they would no longer dictate his present. By learning how to dissolve these past memories, he finally found the technique to heal his body by clearing his mind.

You can also apply this powerful technique when distress stems from a past event. This technique is designed to overcome these patterns. By applying this potent technique, you can shift the way your mind holds onto painful memories. You do not have to be a victim of your history; these mental imprints can be altered. Let's explore this technique:

1. Sit in a quiet place and gently close your eyes.
2. Try to recall a painful event from your past.
3. Imagine it as a movie being played in front of your mind's eye. As you recall the event, identify the exact moment it reaches its peak—the point of deepest pain. At that moment, freeze the scene, as if you were pausing a video at a specific frame. For example, if you are reliving a scene where someone is abusing you, catch the frame where the pain feels sharpest and hit "pause" in your mind.

4. Once you have frozen or paused the scene, it is time to "decorate" it. Begin by mentally decorating the frame. Just as you might use a photo editor to add fun elements to a picture, start changing the components of this painful memory to make it look funnier.

   For example, you may have seen how children play with images of celebrities or models in a magazine. If you give a child a pen, they might doodle a beard and mustache on a glamorous face or turn someone into a funny cartoon. You are going to do exactly the same thing. You are looking at a painful snapshot from your past—a scene you have already frozen in place. Now it is your turn to pick up the mental pen.

   You will now start decorating that scene. Mentally draw a jagged mustache on the face of the person insulting you. You can even give them a pirate's eye patch or turn them into a clumsy cartoon character. As you keep looking at this new version, the image that used to terrify you will be replaced by this absurd caricature. The painful memory will begin to fade. Now take a deep breath and release it, as though releasing the negative energy, and slowly open your eyes. When you open your eyes, you will experience a sense of lightness and even amusement.

5. After a while, replay the same event. Then ask yourself, "Am I still feeling the same intensity of pain I felt just a few minutes ago?" Most certainly, the intensity has diminished. You will begin to feel the liberation that comes from finally being free of that emotional burden.

Occasionally, you might feel stuck in pain when revisiting these memories. In such situations, set a timer to help you step out of that state. This acts as a safety net, ensuring you do not get lost in the emotion. Practice this exercise for a few days, and you will find it easier to step back into the present.

Through this practice, you will realize that you do not need to wait forty years for painful memories to fade. Here and now, in this moment, you have the power to transform your painful memories into something light and even humorous. By doing so, those old images lose their sting. The impact of that event will gradually fade as it is now being viewed in a new way.

When we replay an old, painful record over and over, we reinforce that event and intensify the pain. However, when we view the event in a new way, a new record is created in our mind. We forget the old record.

We all carry different stories because we were raised differently and have undergone our own sets of stressful events. Treat these memories like a film and become the director. Watch the scene in slow motion, then try fast-forwarding through the pain, just like children would play with a video. At other times, just rewind or reverse the order of events. When you rewind a moving picture, it appears like a comedy strip. By turning your stress into such a comedy strip, you break its emotional grip and reclaim your peace of mind.

By practicing this technique, you can process the painful chapters of your story and lighten the load. You no longer need to carry the heavy weight of the past as you sail toward your future.

Action plan:

Process any one of your painful memory using meditation given in this chapter.

19

Inner Peace Amid Stress

Stress and breathing are interconnected.
To quiet the storm within during stress,
learn the art of controlling your breath through meditation.

In a stressful situation, when your mind is overwhelmed by a storm of thoughts, the dust from the storm clouds the mirror of the mind, obscuring the present moment. During such a time, patiently wait and watch the storm till it subsides naturally. Do not try doing anything, and do not be troubled by the thought of how not to do anything. Simply be! Let us understand how to achieve this inner state with an example.

When a ship is caught in a storm and cannot steer through it, the captain drops the anchor into the water. This anchor keeps the ship in place until the storm recedes. This period is the time for doing nothing—the time of unconditional waiting. The captain waits until the weather clears so it can sail safely. If the captain still tries to sail instead of waiting, the ship might overturn and sink.

Similarly, when you are caught in a storm of problems and your faith falters, it is better to wait and do nothing until you receive further indications. Simply, witness your thoughts. Observe the waves of your thoughts from the standpoint of a detached witness, letting them pass by without clinging to any. By witnessing thoughts this way, you shift your focus away from the problem, weaken the power of negative thoughts, and gradually your lost faith begins to be revived. This act of witnessing is a state of doing nothing. From this place of witnessing, the reinforcement of thoughts ceases. Otherwise, the mind clings to thoughts and refuses to let go.

The art of calming the mind through Yoga Nidra

The health of the body affects the mind. A stress-free body nurtures a stress-free mind, while a weak and stressed body becomes a breeding ground for worry. Therefore, practice the art of relaxing the body and mind through Yoga Nidra. Just as animals instantly relax when they feel stressed, we should also learn the art of relaxing our body.

Just as it is essential for every part of our body to get exercise, it is equally vital for every part to receive rest. 70 percent of our stress and fatigue is centered around our eyes. Therefore, at the end of each day, whether sitting or lying down, instruct your eyes, "Release all the stress held around my eyes." When you feel exhausted and want to rest, tell your eyes, "Let go of the stress." Our eyes respond to what we say. Hence, shortly after giving these instructions, you will feel refreshed. You may not have tried this before, but when you do, you will be amazed by the results.

Pranayama is also used for relaxation. For example, inhale for four counts and exhale for six counts. This controlled breathing is beneficial for overall health and relaxation. Pranayama, with its rhythmic breath control, helps balance oxygen levels and effectively release carbon dioxide from the body.

The following practice of Yoga Nidra is also helpful for relaxation.

1. Lie down straight. Take a deep breath and exhale slowly.
2. Gently, rhythmically, and with love, guide each part of your

body to relax. When you instruct, "Relax, let go of the stress," the body responds by releasing the stress it has built up.

3. Starting from your feet, moving up to your head, relax every part of your body. Release stress from your feet, knees, waist, shoulders, and hands. Let the tightness melt away from your back and eyes. Allow your entire body to sink into a state of complete relaxation.
4. Now, to help you relax and calm your mind, visualize a place you love the most. It could be a serene garden, a beautiful mountain stream, or a vast ocean, and so on.
5. Let your mind's eye wander through this scene. Soak in every detail of the scene.
6. Once your mind has fully experienced the scene, bring your awareness back to your body. Scan your body. If you find any lingering tension, gently stretch that part of your body and then release. Softly tell that part of your body, "Release the tension... let it go… relax... relax... relax."
7. This method is highly effective for deep relaxation. Remain in this state for a few minutes. Allow the stillness to settle into your body.

By consciously relaxing each part of your body, you can unlock greater energy and efficiency, allowing you to work longer and achieve more than ever before.

Action plan:

Practice Yoga Nidra for some time.

20

Develop Stress-Coping Habits in Children

Managing pressure and delivering your best performance while staying cheerful in a stressful situation is achieved with relentless practice.

Some people wonder: How do expert players perform in a packed stadium? The whole nation has its eyes on them. Some criticize them for not performing well, while opponents make such comments to disturb them, causing them to lose the game. How do they manage to perform under such high-pressure situations? How did they develop the ability to withstand such intense stress?

The truth is that these players did not become resilient overnight. They practiced enduring such pressure for many years. Gradually, they developed a relaxed attitude in such situations and steadily progressed, climbing the ladder of success one step at a time.

In ancient times, people used to create "poison maidens" to kill their enemies. These girls were given small amounts of poison from childhood, so their bodies were conditioned to it. When the girls grew up, they became poison girls, groomed to kill their enemies. From this example, we can understand that just as a human body can absorb poison, it can also absorb stress in small amounts. If a person is exposed to stress in small doses, they can gradually adapt to it over time and become more resilient.

In the same way, parents should train their children to gradually cope with stress from an early age. Studies show that children who cannot cope with the ups and downs of life are more prone to depression. The rise in suicide cases among children due to stress is linked to a lack of stress handling training in childhood, and also to children becoming victims of wrong beliefs. Resilience is a vital skill that empowers children to navigate life's challenges with confidence and adaptability. Parents can play a crucial role in equipping children with the necessary training.

Let us understand, with some examples, how parents unknowingly instill negative beliefs in children from a young age, leading them to perceive everything negatively and causing stress later in life. The words and actions of elders leave a deep impression on children's tender minds, that creates difficulties later in life.

1. Anaya was the youngest in her family. Her elder sister, Riya, was married into a wealthy family and often mentioned that they had house helpers for everything—right from cleaning and cooking to other household chores. Unconsciously, Anaya internalized the belief that household work was menial, meant for servants, and that she should not have to do it. When she got married and moved into a new home where she had to do all the chores herself, she found it increasingly stressful because her mindset had been conditioned against it. A simple belief filled Anaya's life with immense stress.

2. Sudha and Usha were sisters born into a family of musicians. Both their parents were inclined toward music, and the girls followed suit. While Sudha excelled in classical singing, Usha had a unique talent for fusion music. Because of her melodious voice and relentless dedication, Sudha gained immense fame at a very young age. Their parents and neighbors, consciously or unconsciously, began comparing

> Sudha and Usha, leaving Usha feeling inferior. She wondered, "Why am I not as famous as Sudha? People don't love me; I can't sing like Sudha?" Such thoughts, along with other insecurities, began to take root in her mind.

Nowadays, the word "stress" is used casually in every household for almost everything. Children hear their father say, "I'm under a lot of stress because of work," or their mother say, "I'm stressed because the housework is never-ending." Even their surroundings reinforce phrases like "Stress levels are increasing these days."

As a result, children lose their sensitivity and begin to view stress as a normal part of life. Later, they label every small or big issue as stress, turning it into a status symbol. They believe that experiencing stress means they are working hard and therefore are important.

They begin to say, "I am stressed about my studies," even though studying should be a joyful journey of growth and development. Therefore, it is the responsibility of parents to train their children to live joyfully, even in today's increasingly stressful environment.

Parents can assign small duties to their children promptly and deliberately. Many parents instill the habit of completing small projects in their children effectively from a young age. They use charts, stars, or point systems to reward achievements. Once children accumulate enough points, they receive a small gift or get to visit their favorite place. These activities help children develop a sense of responsibility from an early age while ensuring that work never feels like a burden or a source of stress.

For instance, parents can assign simple tasks, like inflating balloons and tying them to designated spots, within a set time during birthday parties, without shouting or losing patience. If the child shouts at anyone, they lose their points. This teaches them two important lessons: how to complete a task effectively and how to work calmly under pressure without losing their temper. Parents should strive to be the right role models for their children so that children receive the right training to manage their stress from a young age.

Let's understand, with yet another beautiful example, why it is essential to experience small stresses from childhood and use them as stepping-stones to move ahead in life.

> Adarsh was an excellent skater, but whenever he participated in a competition, he could not perform to his full potential. Every time, his mother would ask, "When there is no competition, you skate so well. You cover more distance in a short time, and your speed is incredible. But what happens to you during a competition?"
>
> Adarsh innocently replied, "As soon as I see Daniel ahead of me in the skating rink, I feel stressed and feel like I am going to lose."
>
> His mother then explained, "Look at the legend of cricket, Sachin Tendulkar, or tennis champion, Sania Mirza. They all play under immense pressure to meet the expectations of millions of people across the country and the world. Despite that, they put in their best efforts and delivered outstanding performances. Sachin Tendulkar did not become the world's best batsman overnight. He gradually progressed from small matches like the Ranji Trophy to international cricket, handling stress at every stage. You, too, need to learn to use this stress as a stepping-stone to move forward. Managing pressure and delivering your best performance while staying cheerful in front of others requires practice. In fact, that is far more important than even winning at the skating race."

Today, children need to be told that the small stresses they face in life come to help them grow and improve. Instead of fearing stress, they should embrace it as an opportunity to hone their skills and progress toward their goals.

Action plan:

Identify negative beliefs instilled in you since childhood that are causing you stress. Contemplate how you can use them as a stepping-stone to move ahead in life.

21

Assess Your Stress Level

Since stress is not so much about the event itself as about your perspective, change your perspective and the harmful impact of stress will reduce on your physical well-being.

Today, it is hard to imagine anyone who does not experience stress. Everyone, from youth to the elderly, is dealing with some form of stress whether it is financial, strained relationships, or health concerns. People are trapped in a web of stress.

Today, many youngsters live under the shadow of family discord. They are stressed about their career. In a world where everyone craves status, respect, and a stable career, parents often project their unfulfilled dreams onto their children. This burden leaves the youth caught in a cycle of anxiety, wondering whether they will ever truly live up to their parents' expectations.

To alleviate this stress, many youngsters succumb to addictions and get trapped in a vicious cycle. Addictions are not limited to intoxicating substances like alcohol or drugs. Excessive use of mobile games, endless chats, binge-watching web series, or the midnight lure of social media have become modern compulsions. People feel restless without them, and their non-availability also causes stress.

Besides this, today's children are also growing up in a stressful environment. Often, they are compared to their siblings and pressured to emulate their siblings' successes. Furthermore, the friction of a troubled marriage—where parents argue frequently—leaves children feeling deeply unsettled. The greatest stress among children stems from studies and fierce competition. Those who do not plan their studies from the beginning of the year also experience severe stress during the time leading up to their exams.

It is deeply saddening that suicide cases among the younger generation and children are increasing, highlighting the extreme levels of stress they face. In India alone, nearly 171,418 people committed suicide in 2023, out of which student suicides accounted for 8.1% of the total suicides reported in the year. (Source: National Crime Records Bureau (NCRB))

Apart from children and youth, adults face their own set of stresses. Parents worry about how to raise their children properly amid countless distractions.

On the other hand, women managing households also navigate a world of constant stress. Their mornings are a whirlwind of responsibility—getting children ready for school, preparing multiple meals, and managing the health and medications of the elderly. This weight of responsibility is a shared human experience. Doctors, teachers, businesspeople, and even the retired grapple with their own anxieties. Ultimately, stress does not discriminate; it finds a home in every profession and every stage of life.

Following is a short stress test to identify the factors causing stress in your life. Below is a list of events. Circle the numbers corresponding to the events that have occurred in your life over the past two months.

Sr. No.	Event	Impact
1	Death of a Spouse/Partner	100
2	Divorce	73
3	Marital separation	65
4	Imprisonment	63
5	Death of a beloved family member	63
6	Personal injury or illness	53
7	Strained marriage	50
8	Being laid off or fired at work	47
9	Marital reconciliation	45
10	Retirement	45
11	Decline in family member's health	44
12	Pregnancy	40
13	Sexual challenges	39
14	Arrival of a new family member	39
15	Business reorganization	39
16	Change in financial status	38
17	Death of a close friend	37
18	Difficulties due to changes in the workplace	36
19	Increased arguments with spouse	35
20	Taking a large amount of mortgage	31
21	Changes in job responsibilities	29
22	Children moving out	29
23	Problems with in-laws	29
24	Need for personal achievement	28
25	Starting or closing down a business	26
26	Starting or finishing school / college	26
27	Change in living conditions	25
28	Reviewing and altering personal habits	24
29	Difficulties with the manager at work	23
30	Changes in working conditions or working hours	20
31	Change of residence	20
32	Change of college / university	20

33	Changes in religious activities	19
34	Changes in social activities	18
35	Major weather changes	17
36	Changes in sleep pattern	16
37	Changes in frequency of family gatherings	15
38	Changes in eating and drinking habits	15
39	Vacation	13
40	Festival celebrations	12
41	Minor arguments	10
42	Small Debt	10

Calculate your stress level

Once you have circled the event numbers, sum up the "Impact" scores associated with them to determine your stress level. These impact numbers are based on the severity of the events. For example, if you circled events 5, 8, 20, and 36, your total score would be: 63 + 47 + 31 + 16 = 157. Based on your total impact score, use the chart below to determine your stress level.

Score	Stress Level
Up to 150	Boredom-related stress
150 to 250	Ideal level of stress
250 to 300	Stress is present but still safe
300 to 450	Unsafe level of stress
450+	Very dangerous stage of stress

This assessment offers a glimpse into your stress level, but is not 100% accurate. Since stress is not so much about the event itself as about your perspective, change your perspective and the harmful impact of stress will reduce on your physical well-being.

Action plan:

Conduct stress test for yourself and identify the factors causing you stress.

SECTION III

Underlying Causes and Solutions for Stress

22

The Purpose of Life on Earth

True success is achieved when you attain your life's purpose while observing a fast from stress.

The root cause of human stress is that we have become so absorbed in, consumed by, and attached to worldly affairs that we have forgotten the true purpose of our life. We have lost sight of the very reason why we came to Earth in the first place. In reality, we were meant to lead a happy life here, but instead, we often experience sorrow and stress. Let's explore this through a hypothetical scenario.

> There was a temple nearby. Hearing the chime of the temple bells, you instinctively walked toward the sound. A large crowd had gathered outside the temple. People were standing in long queues, waiting for their turn to catch a glimpse of the temple deity, holding colorful flower garlands of various sizes. You also bought a garland and joined the queue. You saw most of the people leaving the temple looking stressed, weary, and dejected. Only a few had smiles on their faces. Seeing this, you also felt tense.

As you entered the temple, you were taken aback. There was only one idol of the Divine, while the rest were statues of various animals like an elephant, mouse, lion, crow, donkey, horse, wolf, dinosaur, snake, and more. The priest would take each garland, measure its length, and then place it around the animal's neck where it fit well. Obviously, when someone saw their garland fitting around the neck of an elephant, mouse, cat, or donkey instead of the Divine, they felt devastated and left the temple feeling sad. Only a few people came out happy, with their garlands perfectly fitting the Divine. Some people asked the priest why this was happening and learned the reason.

A path to understanding the truth unfolds for those who ask questions. They begin to understand exactly where they went wrong and, more importantly, what they must change in their own lives to set things right. Pause and contemplate: What was it that enabled only a few people to genuinely surrender their garlands to the Divine?

The world is home to various creatures, including animals, birds, insects, sea creatures, etc. Yet the most significant creation of all is the human body which is that very garland to be offered in the above analogy. In reality, God wished to experience His own creation through a human form. Therefore, He created this human body-mind equipped with intellect and discernment. He also set a clear purpose for human life on Earth to realize His divine nature through them, express His divine qualities like love, joy, and peace, and to attain the highest goal of life without stress.

However, the reality is quite different. We have lost sight of our true purpose, blinded by the glitter of the modern world. We are living a stressful life, caught between the shadows of the past and anxieties of the future. Due to this constant stress, the garland of our life has become distorted. It no longer fits the Divine; instead, it ends up around the neck of an animal in the analogy above. This signifies that rather than being aligned with the Divine, we are entangled in worldly illusions and have strayed from our true purpose on Earth.

Life on Earth is meant to serve as a training ground. For that purpose, some events, a degree of stress, and various relationships are attached to our body, the garland. By navigating these, we are supposed to learn our lessons so we can mature and embody the divine qualities wisely. These challenges are designed to teach us the fine art of balancing, allowing our body, mind, and intellect to become fully trained and express the divine qualities. Our garland would then become a perfect fit for the Divine. In this state of alignment, God experiences the world through us, and our purpose on Earth is finally fulfilled.

While God created many other creatures, none are gifted with the mind and intellect that humans possess. All creatures experience stress, but they only use it briefly for survival or defense. Once they overcome danger, they return to their natural state and move on with their lives.

Have you ever seen an animal worried about where its next meal will come from, stressed about providing for its family, or managing its home? Of course not!

An elephant consumes nearly a hundred pounds of food at a time. Yet it is not worried about its next meal. Birds raise their young ones until they are ready to fly, then part ways without the stress of moving on. Even in the wild, when a predator hunts prey, the prey experiences intense stress to survive. It uses that stress as a source of strength to defend itself, and once the danger is averted, it returns to a stress-free state. Nature instilled stress as a positive force; however, humans have turned it into a negative force.

Now, ensure that the stress in your garland, body, remains balanced—neither too much nor too little. Those with a hyperactive nature tend to work under constant stress, which distorts their garland, making it too large for the Divine. On the other hand, people with a lethargic nature find it nearly impossible to begin any task. They prefer to remain idle until a literal earthquake forces them to move. Their garland shrinks so much that it only fits a mouse.

To maintain perfect balance, especially during stressful moments, observe a Stress Fast with this understanding. Just as fasting from food helps the body reset and cleanse, fasting from stress allows us to find clarity and rejuvenate. When stressed, deliberately stay away from it and calmly perform your work, then your body-mind becomes balanced and virtuous. A virtuous body holds onto the right amount of stress needed in any situation, neither more nor less. Such a garland fits perfectly around the Divine. Pause for a minute and contemplate: How fit is your garland to be offered to the Divine today?

When we maintain the perspective and understanding to cleanse ourself internally by eradicating our tendencies and impurities as we go through every small or big event, we begin a journey of true transformation, and our garland finally fits perfectly for the Divine.

If you were told based on how you are living today, your garland is destined for the neck of an animal, you would be shocked. That realization would serve as a wake-up call, making you think, "If this is what's in store for me, I'd better start working on it immediately."

Those who lack this vision keep wandering in the dark. But from now on, your goal should be crystal clear: "My garland must fit the neck of the Divine alone." After that, all your actions will be guided by this goal. This clarity and vision will give your life direction and the strength to overcome stress.

Once you realize that every life event is meant to cultivate divine qualities like love, joy, peace, balance, and faith within you, your approach to challenges will change. So, from now on, whenever a stressful situation arises, remind yourself, "This is an opportunity to shape my garland, making it worthy of the Divine."

Action plan:

Contemplate: How fit is your garland to be offered to the Divine today?

Master of Siddhartha
Refer to this book by Sirshree for deeper understanding

23

Learn From a Robot

When you reflect upon your existential essence
and realize who you truly are through your own experience,
it becomes possible to view stress in a new light.

In today's world, almost everyone has heard of, read about, or seen a robot. When a robot is built, it is programmed with many functions and performs tasks according to those instructions. It is operated by software managed by its controller. It executes only the specific tasks fed into its software; it cannot do anything beyond that.

In a way, our body also functions like a robot. It operates as long as the software called "consciousness" is associated with it. The body stops functioning when consciousness disconnects from it. It becomes a corpse, serving no further purpose. The greatest irony is that, even though everyone knows this fundamental truth, they refuse to accept it and spend their entire lives believing they are the body.

The truth is that this body-mind mechanism is a gift designed and entrusted to us to express the qualities of the Divine; it is nothing more than a robot. To keep this machine running, along with various traits, the quality of stress has been programmed into it, which acts as the drive to get things done. With this understanding, what kind of relationship will you form with the robot of your body-mind?

The understanding is that you are not the body; rather, you are the one using the body to express qualities of the Divine. Therefore, always remember that the body is a robot, not you. You are the one operating the robot, separate from it. To bring harmony between the robot and the software, you need to befriend your body-mind and make it your companion.

So far, you have dealt with your body by assuming, "I am this body; I have to complete these tasks, so I feel stressed." But in reality, the body is your companion that experiences stress, not you. Just as you help a friend in distress, help your body too. Ask yourself, "What is triggering stress in my body, and how can it be handled? My companion is under stress. How can I help it?"

At the same time, strive to know who you really are—the real "I" that exists beyond the body-mind. As you understand that you are separate from the body-mind, you will learn to turn your stress into strength and use it to your advantage. Essentially, the onset of stress actually signifies the generation of power. Whenever you face a challenging or new task, you need power to complete it. Therefore, you feel stressed to generate that power. Once the task is completed, the stress dissipates on its own.

> For instance, imagine there is a race where all athletes are standing at the starting line. The air is filled with tension. As soon as the whistle blows, the athletes run with all their might. Despite the intense stress, they exert their full strength and outpace their compatriots. Once they cross the finish line, their stress subsides. Their stress fueled the power they needed to run. Once the race ends, the stress ends too.

Sometimes, you feel stressed from recalling a past event or worrying about an uncertain future. However, you need not be stressed about it. This body-mind robot is equipped with two magical memory cards that record all its actions. The first magic memory card records your past. Whatever incidents you go through daily, from morning till night, are recorded on this card as they become the past. This memory card never runs out of space as the storage is unlimited.

Whenever you feel stressed by recalling an incident from this card or a similar event resurfaces, have this understanding: "There was a lesson for me to learn in that event that I didn't learn then. Now, that event, or a similar event, has resurfaced not to haunt me, but to teach me that lesson. I must learn it." Harness this magical memory card to shift your perspective to deal with the current events, so you can learn your lessons and dissolve stress with this new wisdom.

The second magical card is the blueprint of your future. Every dream you hold, and a vision or wish for your life, is saved here. Each desire is recorded on this card, and when the right moment arrives, it manifests in your reality.

These two memory cards are recorded, so you can leverage them to reduce the stress in the present. To achieve this, remove A, B, and C from these magical cards. A is stored in the future card, and B and C are stored in the past card.

- A: Anxiety for the future.
- B: Bitterness, the desire for revenge for what was done to you.
- C: Condemnation, guilt, a feeling of regret for what has already transpired.

While anxiety is predominantly linked to uncertainties about the future, the emotions of guilt and revenge are rooted in the past. Guilt is the lingering residue of self-blame, while bitterness or revenge is the burning residue of anger, a silent demand for retaliation.

Learn lessons from your past mistakes and apply those new insights to your advantage in the present. If you harbor guilt or revenge for your past mistakes, practice forgiveness to erase those feelings from your past memory card. Set yourself free by forgiving others, yourself, and seeking forgiveness where needed for your past. Trust that whatever happened was meant to teach you a lesson, and whatever you desire for the future will surely be fulfilled.

Whatever desires you record on your future card will manifest into reality. Hence, do not worry about whether you will have enough food or money to survive. These things will naturally come to you. Learn to use these magical cards and develop your power of imagination. Have faith in nature and its divine timing. To achieve this, adopt the faith formula: **"Whatever is being served to me is meant for my highest good, and I unquestioningly trust the flow of life."**

Just as nature ensures that a newborn receives milk as soon as they are born, nature cares for all living beings by meeting their needs. Every living being lives with this innate faith in nature and receives what they need. Only humans tend to lack faith; now is the time to reclaim it.

Stop resisting the divine flow by denying what is being given to you, as it is meant for your highest good, to help you learn your life lessons, and to dissolve the ties of karmic bondage. Accept these gifts gracefully so you can become free from your karmic bondage. By knowing you are not the body, you can realize who you truly are and attain the sole purpose of coming to earth.

Action plan:

1. Whenever stress arises, observe it with the understanding that it is with the body, not with you. The body is your companion that experiences stress, not you.
2. In situations where the mind resists, try applying the faith formula.

Who am I Now
Refer to this book by Sirshree for deeper understanding

24

The Trap of Attachment

Let there be love, not attachment.
Love sets you free, while
attachment only tethers you to stress.

When we develop a deep bond with a person or an object, care for them with love, and stay mindful of them, we feel energized, confident, and secure. This nurturing awareness, in its purest form, is love. However, when this love exceeds its limits, we feel worried about separation from that person or object, or fear losing them. This excessive clinging turns pure love into attachment, which then becomes a cause of stress. Let's understand this with an example.

> Parth applied for jobs at many companies and attended some interviews without stress. But one day, he received a call for an interview from a top-tier firm, and he suddenly felt, "I should get selected in this company." Until this point, he approached interviews without getting attached to any specific outcome. However, he developed an attachment to this firm, and his detached approach was replaced by anxiety and stress. He felt stressed, "Will they hire me or not?"

This explains how attachment to outcomes or objects causes stress by disrupting life's natural flow. While nature operates in a state of free flow, humans struggle to hoard and control every experience, claiming it as "mine." This desperate urge to own and control is the root cause of stress.

Attachment can act as a silent saboteur. Often, parents give in to every whim of their children due to excessive attachment. Later, even when they notice their children drifting toward the wrong path, they find themselves helpless and powerless to intervene. Some people become so attached to their relationships that they try to hold on to them and control. This creates a sense of suffocation for their loved ones, leading to rifts, causing deep-seated resentment and stress. Ultimately, they become a barrier to the growth and development of their loved ones.

Many times, people find it hard to leave a certain place. If it is their ancestral property, they feel compelled to stay for generations just to preserve it and safeguard a legacy. They resist change, even when it means living in a cramped, confined space for years. This shows an attachment to that place. Likewise, some people refuse to leave their workplace, while others are attached to some objects, possessions, or even a particular sport. Let's understand how a hobby meant for relaxation can quickly turn into a source of agitation.

> Kapil started watching a cricket match on TV just for entertainment. But soon he got completely drawn in, and before he knew it, he was feeling stressed out. He was overwhelmed with thoughts. "What's going to happen now? Who will win? My team must win." What began as a source of joy quickly turned into a source of worry. He started swearing at the players and shouting at his kids to be quiet.

Why did this happen? What caused such intense stress?

When he started watching the game, he was neither attached to the game nor any team. Both teams were equal in his eyes. But somewhere along the way, he became emotionally attached to one team. He did not realize when the shift occurred. We have never been trained how to watch a game or live life with healthy detachment. Such is human nature, the irony of life turning simple pleasures into sources of immense stress!

These external attachments, be it to places or possessions, are visible and can be overcome. However, the deepest of all attachments lies with our own body. Although we know that this body is transient and will eventually die, we firmly believe that we *are* the body till the final moments of life with the body, mourning its departure. This attachment to the body is so strong and deep-seated that even a minor illness or injury can trigger a surge of stress in us and those around us.

Even though we know that "Nothing should be held onto, for everything must be left here on Earth," the sense of "I," "Me," and "Mine" triggers attachment. Therefore, understand that we have come to Earth for a short visit. Everything is meant to be used, not possessed, even this body! When the time comes to let them go, do so gracefully and happily because they were meant to be relinquished.

In essence, to lead a stress-free life, allow things and people to come and go. Stay in a state of free-flow and detachment where you are not attached to any people, objects, or outcomes. This detachment is the remedy to grief, worry, and stress, paving the way for inner peace.

Every morning when you wake up, remind yourself of the truth with this prayer:

"I am not this body.

I am merely its custodian.

May I enter the world each day with a spirit of detachment.

Let me walk through the world,

but let the world not walk through me or influence me.

Let no worldly thing or external force overpower me."

By affirming this daily, we cultivate a detached mindset, enabling us to face life's challenges with calmness and equanimity.

Daily mindfulness practice: The 5-minute reset

Practice the following short meditation every morning.

1. Set a 5-minute timer. Sit in a meditative posture and gently close your eyes. With the understanding that everything in this world is fleeting and will eventually be left behind on Earth, silently affirm:

"O Lord!
I acknowledge that I am not this body.
I am only using it to express divine qualities.
May I connect to all relationships and possessions
while living in a state of detachment.
Please guide me on this path."

2. Remain seated for a few moments, immersed in this sense of detachment. When the timer goes off, express gratitude and gently open your eyes.

Engage in activities while maintaining the sense of detachment. Remember that cultivating detachment is not an overnight process. It requires time and effort. However, with consistent practice, the feeling of detachment and inner peace can be developed.

This meditation helps you remain detached from your body and interact with people and possessions without feeling stressed. When you release identification with your body, detachment from everything else happens naturally. Your illusions begin to dissolve, and you begin to realize who you truly are.

Action plan:

1. Reflect on your attachments.
2. Practice mindfulness meditation daily in the morning.

Detachment From Attachment
Refer to this book by Sirshree for deeper understanding

25

Empty Your Sacred Altar

The most effective way to find lasting peace from stress is to bring your beliefs into the light of conscious awareness. One of the most significant beliefs to address is, "I am the body."

A man wanted to perform a sacred fire ritual at his house, so he brought a metal container to serve as the altar. He wanted to light a sacred fire in it and offer oblations to the Divine. Since he had to procure more supplies for the ritual, he left the fire altar in the courtyard and went away.

A short while later, a crow flew by carrying a piece of meat in its beak. Accidentally, the meat slipped from its beak and fell directly into the fire altar. Soon after, a passerby mistook the fire altar for a trash bin and threw a banana skin into it. Later, everyone passing through the courtyard treated it as a trash bin and dumped their trash there. What a state the fire altar ended up in! What was meant for a sacred ritual had become a garbage bin, simply because of ignorance.

The situation reached a breaking point when the man returned home. After finishing his meal, he wiped his hands with a tissue and threw it into the same fire altar. It looked like a trash bin to him, too! The fire altar was so full of trash that he did not even realize that it was the altar meant for the sacred fire ritual.

What does this story point to? It explains a profound truth: the human body is also a sacred altar. We carry this body wherever we go. It was given to us for the sacred rituals of acquiring wisdom, performing karma, and practicing meditation. However, much like the man in the story, we, too, have forgotten the true purpose of human life. Consequently, we continue to fill this sacred container with the garbage of beliefs and conditioning that do not serve our true purpose.

Let us understand what beliefs are and how they are formed. A belief is merely a thought or notion we accept as true, even though it is not necessarily the reality or the truth.

God desired to see His own image in a physical form, so He created humans and sent them into the world. He took the beautiful form of a small child and joyfully whispered into their ear, "I created you just like Me." Filled with the same bliss, He sent all children into the world with this message. Every child comes to Earth with the divine purpose: Your body is your sacred altar. To keep it pure, you must fill it with the offerings of wisdom, karma, and meditation***.

Once the child is born, after a few days, the altar of their body is given a name, and from that day on, it is addressed only by that name. This is the very first belief cast into their altar: you *are* this physical body. While the name was initially given for convenience, over time, they become deeply entangled in the root belief that they *are* the body. Just as one lie requires a thousand more to cover it up, countless other limiting beliefs become associated with the root belief, "I am this body."

***To read in further depth about these three precious offerings, read the books *100% Wisdom*, *100% Karma*, and *100% Meditation* by Sirshree.

This is how the sacred altar of the body begins to take the form of a trash bin. Because people perceive it as empty, they feel compelled to fill it with something. It begins to get worse when the child, after about two and a half years of age, having absorbed the voices around them, starts copying them and throwing in their own trash. Parents, teachers, peers, TV, and now even social media contribute to this clutter.

Let's understand how these beliefs are formed with some examples.

1. Rita and Reema were standing at the bus stop waiting to board their kids onto the school bus. There was still some time for the bus to arrive when they saw a sanitation worker sweeping the street. Reema used the moment to warn her child, pointing out the worker, "Look at that. If you don't want to end up doing this kind of work, you'd better study hard and become someone important." On the other hand, Rita told her child, "You must get educated so that you can help people like him and many others. That way, you can build a better world for everyone around you."

   What will happen because of this? One child will study with a sense of purpose, inspired by the idea of building a better society. The other child, however, will feel pressured to achieve high grades, fearing they might become someone they consider inferior. Unknowingly, parents instill such beliefs from a tender age, creating a sense of disgust for low-profile workers and their work. Later, this belief becomes a source of deep-seated stress and a significant barrier to the child's true progress.

2. At school, a teacher asked a student to write something on the board. The student started writing, but the chalk kept breaking, and he kept holding the duster upside down. The entire class burst into laughter. Later, during a fancy-dress competition, the same student tripped while climbing onto the stage, and once again, everyone laughed. From these painful incidents, a limiting belief took root in him, "I am

not meant for the stage," and eventually he stopped going on stage or even answering in class.

His innocent mind began to internalize the belief that people laugh at the weak and that he is one of them. When he encountered such an incident for the first time, a belief took root: "If I am a loser or make a mistake, people will mock me." Even when people laughed for a different reason, not related to him, he would think, "Everyone is laughing at me. They are talking about me." He believed the world was judging every move he made. Due to this deeply ingrained belief rooted in childhood, he chose to be stressed over trying new things. Fear and his limiting beliefs overshadowed his aspirations to perform and gain recognition. He forgot that weakness was a temporary phase he could overcome and that mistakes were part of learning and growth.

Eliminating stress at its root requires uncovering deeply ingrained beliefs. If you truly value freedom, it is essential to bring those beliefs to light. Contemplate the thoughts and assumptions you hold about others or the world at large. Look deep within to identify the core thought, or the underlying negative belief that triggers your stress.

The definition of stress can vary from person to person; it is not the same for everyone. It fluctuates based on everyone's beliefs. Some feel stressed about money, some about health, some about the future, and others about work. Whatever beliefs one holds most strongly cause the greatest stress.

For instance, in India, a son choosing his life partner without the family's consent can cause intense stress for the parents. This happens because their core beliefs are built on the rigid pillars of caste, community, and religion. When those boundaries are crossed, it becomes a nightmare for them. They feel, "Come what may, but this should not happen." While those who have risen above such prejudices might find this outlook irrational, for families still holding onto such beliefs, it is a significant source of stress. Once this belief is challenged, a vicious cycle of stress may begin within the family.

Deeply reflect on every area of your life and ask yourself, "What specific belief triggers my anxiety and stress about the future?" Once you find the answer and bring each of these beliefs to light, you will be amused and laugh at the realization, "I can't believe I was ruining my life over such a trivial belief."

Therefore, resolve to step out of every limiting belief, even the most fundamental one, "I am the body." Take steps to free yourself from this belief and experientially know that you are not the body, so you can use your body as a sacred altar for spiritual growth and fulfillment rather than as a trash bin for beliefs. Only then will you begin to experience the bliss of true freedom.

We have learned that beliefs cause stress, but there is a deeper belief about stress itself within us: Stress has taken hold of us. We believe that stress, worries, or anxieties have trapped us, but the reality is that we are the ones holding on to stress. The good news is that we inherently possess the power to release it. The moment we consciously realize who is holding whom, we see that we are the ones clinging to stress. This realization itself will help us break free from it. It is all about loosening the grip on what we have been holding on to from within.

Hence, it is essential to understand that we are the ones holding on to stress. No feeling can hold onto us; it simply exists. We often convince ourselves we are victims and tell others, "This happened; that person did this to me." The key lies in understanding who is holding onto the feeling. By repeatedly dwelling on that incident, we keep it and its associated stress alive. When you see this clearly, you gain the power to let go. Follow the techniques in this book to release your stress, one by one, so you can enjoy a life of freedom, unburdened by false beliefs and tension.

Action plan:

Reflect on your limiting beliefs. Resolve to be free from them and to use your body as a sacred altar for spiritual growth and fulfillment.

26

Remain Empty During Your Free Time

Build the foundation of your life by being truly empty in your moments of emptiness.

Have you ever noticed how you go through events as they unfold? If you observe carefully, you will realize that there is constant stress within you. Our mind is accustomed to stressing over every little thing.

For instance, if you are traveling somewhere, the internal chatter begins, "Will my work get done? Will the train be on time? If it arrives, will I be able to find a seat? If I get to sit, will I reach my destination on time? If I reach my destination, will someone be there to pick me up?"

In this way, the mind somersaults in every situation throughout the day. Moreover, it drags the senses along. Upon closer observation, we will find that our senses are always eager to know what will happen next. They are always trying to leap into the unpredictable future, causing anxiety. While this effort is not visible on the outside, this inner mechanism is always at play. The eyes, ears, and tongue, for instance, want to leap forward into the next experience, but they are compelled to stay within the body. This restraint and inner conflict create stress within the senses. Let's understand this in depth.

> Imagine you are looking at a view outside; however, your eyes yearn to leap into the future. They want to see something new—like the latest fashion trends, a trendy mall, new movies, or a new web series. Similarly, while your ears might be listening to the present sounds, your mind intervenes, "Wouldn't it be great to listen to some new music?" Likewise, while your nose is immersed in the scents and aromas around you, the mind calls out, "Is there a new perfume?" or "I smell something delicious being cooked, yummy!"
>
> Meanwhile, your tongue, bored with the same old flavors every day, craves a new taste, fresh gossip, or a bit of backbiting to make life interesting. Without it, life feels monotonous, stuck in a dull, repetitive routine. Even the skin yearns for a new experience. If it is hot, it wants a cool breeze; if it is cold, it craves warmth. It demands new comforts for physical pleasure and so on.

This habitual craving of the senses for something new causes stress within us. To free yourself from this constant stress, develop the art of being empty in your free moments. Indeed, nature offers countless opportunities to simply be a witness and observe the world as it unfolds. However, as our senses tend to rush ahead into the future or habitually search for something new, we do not stay empty during these waiting periods and create stress.

Even when people retreat into nature, they remain stressed. For instance, when they go on a picnic, instead of relaxing, the mind races, "What's the next sightseeing point? Let's hurry up and take a picture here so we can quickly move to the next. Let's move!" The irony is: you go on a picnic to unwind, but your senses keep you on a deadline to tick a checklist. You end up spending the entire day in the same anxious state, due to the restless habit of the senses. The true purpose of a picnic is not about seeing every sightseeing spot on the map; it is about losing oneself in that moment with nature. To truly enjoy it, just sit in quietude, doing nothing, and get absorbed in nature. We must learn this art.

When you visit places like mountains or the seashore, practice the art of simply being empty as you observe. Listen to the melodies of birds, breathe in the unique fragrance of the nearby blossoms, and let the fresh breeze be your companion. Watch the rhythm of the ocean; see the waves rise and fall. Observe how a large wave swells, and the small one follows and eventually dissolves back into the ocean. Simply observe and feel them. In this way, take advantage of every opportunity nature offers to gradually master the art of simply being present.

As you master the art of being truly free, i.e., *simply being* in your quiet moments, a gradual transformation begins that will lead you to a stress-free life. While this can happen in nature, it can also be practiced amid everyday life. Therefore, you must learn to sit in this state.

While at home, take a few moments in between to simply sit and do nothing. Allow yourself brief moments of stillness, free from activity, simply being present. Your senses, driven by habit, will protest, giving rise to restlessness. They will crave action and warn, "If you don't give us something new, we'll jump out and latch onto something." "We want this, we want that," they will demand. When their demands are not met, they will create tension in the body. But now, you must sit still and observe these urges. Remind yourself and check: "Is this stress necessary? Can't I just sit still for a while?"

When you sit in these pockets of silence, without doing anything, your internal state changes. You notice that your senses have stopped craving for new experiences. They are in a state of restful stillness. There is no longer an urge to know or hear something, to see or feel something, no craving to eat, to go somewhere, or to experience something new. As the internal struggle ceases, the stress simply dissolves.

All day long, you listen to your senses and do exactly what they demand. But now, it is time to take charge and train them to be empty during idle moments. You will experience many moments during the day when you have nothing to do. These moments are usually labeled "boredom." In reality, they are a blessing of nature, allowing you to practice stillness.

For example, when someone says, "I'll call you back in five minutes," nature has served this opportunity for your inner transformation. However, the mind does not like being idle, so it immediately urges, "Do something right now. Make a call, grab a magazine, pick up a book, turn on the TV or radio, listen to music, or scroll through the reels on your phone for something new," and so on.

Instead of waiting for something to happen, simply observe what is happening in the present. Notice the subtle tension that arises from the quiet yearning of the mind for "Something must happen." At times, you must simply sit with your eyes open, noticing every nuance of stress that emerges. This is because when the mind sees nothing coming from outside, it wants to close the eyes and search for something within. It starts imagining scenarios, so it has something to hold onto. Hence, keep your eyes open and be in the present moment.

With regular practice, you will discover what it feels like for your senses to stay relaxed and stress-free. This is the essence of mastering the art of living, a state in which the mind and senses are calm and free from unnecessary demands. Make use of every opportunity nature provides and train your senses to remain still during idle time. Over time, this training will lead to a profound transformation in how you experience life. This is the true art of living a stress-free life!

Action plan:

Spend some time doing nothing, simply being in the present.

Power of Present
Refer to this book by Sirshree for deeper understanding

27

Decode the Cues From Nature

Instead of trying to find solutions while under stress,
it is better to reflect well in advance.
With this, you will master the art
of overcoming stress instantly.

Being proactive is an essential skill not just in our daily life, but also for addressing stress. It involves preparing ourselves mentally in advance. By preparing ahead of time, we empower ourselves to face life's inevitable stresses with greater composure and creativity, breaking free from the repetitive cycle of stress and reaction.

Working professionals should anticipate stress before it strikes, since it is an inevitable part of life. They need to adopt a proactive approach and ask themselves, "If I get stressed in this situation, what will I do? Will I panic reactively, or will I respond creatively?"

It is like digging a well long before thirst sets in. If you wait until you are parched to start digging a well, the burden of addressing the situation alongside the crisis becomes overwhelming, leading to frustration.

Rather than searching for solutions in the midst of stress, it is far more effective to strategize for stress when life is calm. We can find more ways to overcome stress when the mind is calm because stress impairs our ability to think logically. Those who reflect on and observe the vicious cycle of rising stress with awareness can truly break free from it. Those who fail to prepare remain unaware and become ensnared in its loop.

Preparation should begin the moment you see a challenge on the horizon. For example, a father knows that Sunday, when the children are home, often brings a certain level of stress. Having experienced many stressful Sundays, he can anticipate challenges and proactively set the stage for a calmer weekend well in advance.

He can visualize the upcoming Sunday in his mind. He is aware of the patterns and how the day is likely to unfold: the phone will ring, the kids will shout and scream, and they will fight over the TV remote to watch their favorite channels. Chaos would be inevitable, but he can plan his responses proactively. He can think through how he will handle the conflicts. How will he communicate with his children? How can he ensure everyone gets what they need? By reflecting and preparing for these moments even before Sunday arrives, he can transform a chaotic day into a harmonious one for the entire family.

Sometimes, despite the best planning, things still go astray. When they do, treat these moments not as failures but as opportunities to reflect and refine your approach. Have faith that such experiences are helping you collectively grow and evolve as a family. Otherwise, without this training, people often become worse over time, deteriorating further. Instead of becoming pure, their mind becomes more clouded and cluttered, and patience wears thin with every passing day. They become more irritable, reactive, or insensitive.

For instance, someone who did not swear before may now casually hurl insults, indicating that they are regressing rather than maturing. Ideally, every life experience should add a layer of maturity and wisdom. However, for those who live without awareness, it is just the opposite. They get worse over time because they are caught in a cycle of mindless living that does not benefit them.

Many students ignore their studies throughout the year, only to cram at the last minute. They often feel overwhelmed by stress. They panic and struggle, forcing themselves to study and somehow manage to get through. But because they do not break the habit, the next exam brings the same suffering all over again, leaving them to succumb to stress, struggle, and barely manage to pass.

In this journey of life, these students learn nothing from their repeated struggles. However, if a student were to dig a well before they feel thirsty, i.e., if they pause to analyze why they feel stressed and plan a different approach, they could break free from this cycle of unnecessary stress and enhance their awareness. This newfound awareness will allow them to move beyond the old reactive habits and consciously experiment with better ways to prepare, turning a source of panic into an opportunity for growth.

For example, they might acknowledge, "I could handle 50% of my stress during this exam. Next time, I'll aim for 75%, if not 100%." Through thoughtful experiments, the student not only learns how to face exams effectively but also prepares themselves to navigate the exams of life itself.

Further, when exam results are due, stress often resurfaces. If the student continues to feel stressed every time, it indicates they have not learned the lessons this stress was meant to teach. Life will bring more tests, challenges, and results, and if they do not break the cycle, they will live a stressful life. To break this cycle, they must ask themselves, "What is this stress trying to teach me? How can this feeling be useful to my growth?" Once they start seeing stress as a learning opportunity and understand its purpose, it stops being a problem and becomes a tool for learning and growth.

Nature has a unique way of teaching lessons by repeatedly presenting the same situations until we learn from them. Once we learn those lessons, those events cease to appear in our life.

For instance, if you find yourself constantly trapped in cycles of hate, it signifies that you have not yet learned the lesson hatred is trying to teach, perhaps to cultivate love. Hatred is an opportunity to understand what love truly is. Every repetition in life offers you another chance: "Learn this time. Learn it now."

Last time, if you struggled with an exam and were stressed about the result, this time, learn to study calmly and focus during the exam. If you do not learn this time, the same event will keep coming back until you do. Nature patiently continues to offer its "Grace" in the form of repeated challenges until the lesson is learned.

> A manager in a company knows that a demanding project is on the horizon. He is aware that the work will require round-the-clock commitment. However, if he has not reflected beforehand on how to handle those days, he will inevitably drift into his old habits, struggling, complaining, and being highly stressed.
>
> But what if he approaches the situation with awareness? Instead of dreading the workload, if he recognizes it as an opportunity, he can see it as a chance to improve his efficiency and develop a stress-free approach. It is an opportunity to progress to the next level in the game of life. People who play video games know the fun of playing at higher levels, where each new level brings faster-paced tasks, more challenges, and demands more awareness.

Stress enhances awareness. Professionals who perform on stage know that the nervousness before stepping onto the stage is natural because it demands heightened alertness. When you are about to undertake a task that requires perfection, you need this heightened state of alertness. "What if something like a machine or equipment does not work? What if the audience reacts poorly?"

In such situations, you need the agility that comes from deep, pre-trained awareness. A wise person will say, "Every challenge strengthens me. These events are training me, helping me get better, so I welcome them." Similarly, someone who thinks about their work in advance will recognize that each upcoming project is not merely a task but an invaluable opportunity. Such projects do not come every day. Recognizing the opportunity, that person will prepare in advance and await those events without stress.

In every situation, assess yourself by asking, "How balanced am I in this moment?" You may set simple reminders, like wearing a rubber band on the wrist, as a physical cue to stay mindful and not get caught up in the moment. The band serves as a reminder that naturally increases your awareness, and amid the tasks, you will remember to stay stress-free. If the band does not serve its purpose, you can try applying a strong odor, fragrance, or a pain-relief balm on the tip of your nose. Even amid a lot of hustle and bustle, the sensation on the nose can remind you that you are working on a special project and need to stay balanced.

Pushing through tasks without awareness, stressing and forcing outcomes, may earn recognition. But it will hold no real meaning, especially if you have not used the process to deepen your awareness. The true purpose is to cultivate awareness because working without awareness will not fulfill the goal of your life.

Many people achieve big things in life through struggle and frustration. They might get the work done by yelling at people, but they never work on the main goal of their life on Earth. They fail to realize the ultimate purpose of life through their work and waste every opportunity. Hence, develop the habit of contemplation in advance. To grow in life, it is important to take time to reflect and prepare consciously.

Action plan:

Identify stressful situations that are repeatedly occuring in your life. Contemplate how you will make them instrumental for your growth.

28

Stress – An Impetus for Growth

You will be able to perceive stress properly only when you learn to see every event as an opportunity.

In today's modern, fast-paced life, we are all plagued by stress related to building a career, finding a job, maintaining healthy relationships, staying fit, balancing responsibilities in married life, and raising children properly. However, beyond these external factors, there is an internal factor that is upsetting us and making our lives hollow. It is the stress caused by our thoughts.

When the stress of thoughts takes hold, even having the world's greatest joys at our disposal would not be enough to make us happy. Let's understand this stress through an analogy of soldiers.

> Imagine a huge prison yard enclosed by towering walls. The gates are heavily guarded. There is no way to escape. Every exit is locked, and every wall is insurmountable. The prison inmates are required to perform various demanding tasks, such as drawing water from the well, gardening, cooking, cleaning, and heavy labor, such as quarrying stone and

chopping wood. These activities lead to frequent physical injuries and chronic pain. Some wounds are acute, while others are healing. Despite the pain, they are compelled to continue their work. During their breaks, they play cards to distract themselves. This is how they lead their lives.

As the prisoners go about their chores, they occasionally see a squad of soldiers marching across the yard. The sight of the soldiers immediately triggers a wave of panic and fear. The prisoners wonder, "Are they here to inflict new wounds?" They remain under immense stress until the soldiers leave. Only after the soldiers leave do the inmates relax and resume their assigned tasks.

The irony is that some of the soldiers the prisoners fear and consider their enemies are actually doctors disguised as soldiers. They are there to treat the prisoners' wounds. However, their stern, rigid demeanor frightens the prisoners, who scream and shout in panic. Consequently, the soldiers simply walk away, leaving the prisoner's wounds untreated.

Let us understand the deeper meaning of this analogy. The prisoners represent us, human beings. The prison represents *Maya*, the illusory world. We become entangled in Maya as we lead our lives. The marching soldiers represent thoughts that invade at will and disrupt our peace, causing us distress.

Just as the prisoners are haunted by fear of soldiers, we are tormented by negative thoughts stemming from past events, such as insults, failures, criticism, or strained relationships, as well as by anxieties about the future. These thoughts resurface intermittently, causing distress. While some good and positive thoughts, symbolized by the doctors disguised as soldiers, do arise, we fail to recognize them. Instead of welcoming them, we treat them as enemies and flee in fear. To seek temporary refuge, we immerse ourselves in occasional distractions or entertainment to escape the pain. But this offers only a fleeting respite, not lasting liberation.

We must take advantage of the doctors disguised as soldiers, i.e., good, positive thoughts, to escape the prison of thoughts. To do this, we need to learn to recognize these doctors and seek help. However, this requires the ability to identify and understand those thoughts. What are they pointing to and what lies behind them? Let us understand this through an example.

> Imagine a street where a crowd has gathered to watch a film shoot. A man steps forward from the crowd and begins moving people aside. However, without understanding his motive, you push him back in self-defense. In reality, he intended to move the crowd aside so that everyone could see the actor they had gathered to see. However, because you were unaware of his motive and did not understand the context of his kindness, you perceived him as a threat and pushed him back.

We do the same thing with our thoughts. Whenever we have to perform a task, a swarm of both positive and negative thoughts surges through our mind. This triggers stress, causing frustration and even anger. In doing so, we miss the solutions and ideas hidden within those thoughts that could lead us to growth and success. But because we lack understanding, we become overwhelmed by stress and choose to wallow in our own unhappiness, ignoring the solution.

Hence, whenever stress arises, remind yourself: "Some ideas are emerging behind these stressful thoughts. The solution will arrive easily if I remain calm and composed." Once you grasp this profound truth, you will begin to see every stressful situation as an opportunity for growth.

Whenever you resist stressful thoughts and question why the stress has come, the solution stops midway and fails to reach you. Henceforth, understand that whatever thoughts pass through you contain the solution; you need to gracefully welcome them. Watch them pass by with great peace as if you have nothing to do with them.

If you can recognize who is hiding behind thoughts, stress will simply dissolve. Problems and progress walk hand in hand. Today's success will inevitably bring forth tomorrow's challenge, and the solution to that challenge will lead to a breakthrough the day after, which in turn will bring forth further challenges. This is the cycle of continuous growth. With this new perspective, how will you view stressful thoughts going forward? They are not enemies; they are simply the force pushing you toward your next level of growth.

Think of stressful thoughts as the crowd at a train station waiting to board the train. People there may push, jostle, or make you uncomfortable, but as soon as the train arrives, they push you inside the train. Without that push, you would never make it through the doors. Imagine someone saying, "I'll wait for everyone to board first, and then I'll get on." By the time they act, the train would have already departed.

Once you understand how nature works, you stop resenting the "push" and start feeling grateful for it. Similarly, in life, stress and challenges are nudges that propel us to act before it is too late.

For instance, when our body starts showing signs like fatigue or pain, it acts as the first push. If we ignore them, we risk missing a warning about a more serious health issue. However, if these symptoms prompt us to seek a checkup, we discover we have narrowly avoided a serious illness.

Nature supports us by presenting problems. We need to only guard our peace, welcome the knocks of life, and learn our lessons. Then the journey of bright growth will start.

Action plan:

Reflect on the incidents that have troubled you and see what solutions, ideas were hidden behind them.

29

Be Together, but Not Within

Train your mind in such a way that
it can remain empty and undisturbed,
even while observing and hearing everything.

Imagine a huge fish tank teeming with thousands of fish of different shapes and colors. In the water, oxygen-filled bubbles are also floating and even communicating with one another. Some of them are constantly shouting and seem distressed. When these screaming bubbles are carefully observed, they are not filled fully with air; instead, they contain flying fish. Some contain ten, some twenty, and others have even forty or more fish. These bubbles are screaming because they are overwhelmed and desperately trying to release the fish they carry, but failing. Some bubbles are calm, behaving gently and gracefully. They seem to have only one fish inside them, the fish of the present moment.

Now, let us understand the deeper meaning of this analogy. The fish symbolize events in a person's life, and the bubbles represent the individual. The bubbles, filled with many fish and their screaming, signify the imprint of stressful events on a person's subconscious mind. Countless events unfold in a person's life each day. They meet various people, and each interaction leaves a mark. They like some people or events, and dislike others. The shadows of all these experiences remain trapped in their mind, causing stress.

However, there are also calm bubbles that represent people who live a stress-free life. This does not mean their lives are devoid of events or challenges. They do face them, but they do not become overly attached to events or allow situations to overwhelm them. An event occurs, thoughts arise, but after a short while, the thoughts subside. The topic is closed for them. They do not dwell on the event or problem for too long. They know how to detach themselves from their thoughts.

You might wonder whether it is possible to shield ourselves from the negative influences of people and events. Is it possible for two people to live under the same roof without letting the other "get under one's skin," i.e., to share a home without internalizing each other's negativity? Can a boss and an employee work together without either carrying the other home in their head?

The truth is, we unknowingly start hoarding experiences from childhood. We keep adding more and more fish to our mental tank without realizing. From childhood events to unnecessary worries about neighbors and relatives, we store and cling to everything, even though it only brings us pain and sorrow. Rarely do we pause to ask ourselves, "What am I gaining by holding on to these painful, troubling thoughts?"

If you want to truly free yourself from stress, pain, and troubles, you must stop letting these "fish"—events and people—enter your inner world, i.e., influence your mind. To do this, you need to understand a simple principle and mantra:

The principle: You must live with people, but you must not internalize them, i.e., you must not let them live inside you.

The mantra: We are together, but not within each other.

Let us understand how to use this principle and mantra.

Our eyes and ears act as highways, allowing events to enter our brain and subconscious mind. Throughout the day, our senses are constantly feeding on external inputs, liking and disliking them. As a result, these "fish"—events, people, and their impressions—make their way into our inner world and get stored there.

> Let's consider a hypothetical scenario. You step out for the day and encounter various people. On your way, you see someone you are instantly drawn to, and they end up at your home. Then you cross paths with a beggar whose appearance repels you, but they, too, end up at your home. You see a cute little child and think, "Wow, such a cute little one!" and that child also ends up in your house. You witness an accident and feel fearful. You see a new, swanky car on the market, and a desire arises to have one like it. You watch advertisements telling you to eat this, wear that, try this lotion, or apply that beauty product. Some you like, some you dislike. Thus, throughout the day, you see many such people and events.
>
> When you return home in the evening, you find them all waiting for you. Your favorite film star, that cute little kid, that dreadful beggar, the car, the traffic, all crowding your mental space. Suddenly, you feel stressed and think, "Wait! Give me a break! Who invited all these people? How did they get in?" They sneaked in through the highways of your eyes and ears, riding the wave of your likes and dislikes.
>
> What will you do now? Will you remove them one by one or all at once? It is difficult to remove all of them at once when they have entered your mental space. Henceforth, before letting them in, apply the wisdom of principle and use the mantra: **"We are together but not within each other."** In other words, walk with the world without letting it live in your head. Leave everything and everyone outside; do not allow them to pile up in your inner world. Leave the day's events exactly where they happened.

> Think of it like visiting a sick friend in the hospital. You sincerely want to help them. But to help, you do not lie down in the bed next to them and undergo the same treatment. Your role is to support them, pray for them, and offer them comfort, then return home. This is the essence of the mantra: We are together but not inside. You are "together, but not inside" the illness. You walk beside them, but do not take the sickness home with you.

Along with the mantra, you can also use a physical gesture, a *mudra,* to stop external events from cluttering your inner space. It is as simple as snapping your fingers and gesturing for someone to leave. When you feel a like or dislike beginning to take root, snap your fingers and signal it to stay outside. This sends a clear physical cue to your brain to let go of anything unnecessary or unimportant. By practicing this, you can learn to co-exist with life's experiences without letting them take over your inner peace.

So, take a moment to reflect: What "fish" are swimming in your mind right now—which events or people have set up camp inside you? Which issues need to be released today? Which thoughts, incidents, or relationships have you still been carrying that are robbing you of your peace?

You may realize it is time to let go of certain thoughts and experiences. You have carried these burdens long enough; they no longer serve a purpose. Whatever incidents have happened and the people you have encountered since childhood still float within you like restless fish. Can you show them the way out today? Can you become like those serene bubbles of the present, light yet inherently peaceful and still?

If the answer is yes, adopt this principle and mantra as your way of life and gradually reduce the number of fish that enter you.

As we go through life, certain things inevitably slip in and start piling up within us. Now we need to become aware of them. Use practices such as meditation, prayer, principles, mantras, and *mudras* to help cleanse the mind. The moment you begin this practice, the process of emptying starts, leading to transformation. You can then firmly resolve, "This is how I will live from now on."

With this, the number of "fish" will reduce, and even if they do, only "fish" of the present will come because you are dealing with people in the present, without carrying the past. This does not mean that stress and sorrow will vanish, or that problems and difficulties will not exist. They will still float around you, but they will not enter you. They will remain external, not robbing you of your peace of mind.

Action plan:

Which thoughts, incidents, or relationships have you still been carrying that are robbing you of your peace? Adopt the principle and mantra to gradually reduce them.

30

My Self Am Present

Instead of focusing on stress,
use words that promote joy and wisdom.
This will create a new cycle of happiness
and break the old vicious cycle.

We have read about the brain's reaction to stress and its negative consequences. Our brain has incredible power; it can accomplish tasks effortlessly without stress. However, the moment we use words like "stress" or similar phrases such as "there is too much work," "the future is uncertain," "when will this be done," "when will we have our own house," "when will the problems be solved," "when will the children grow up," "we don't have this," "we don't have that," the brain gets into overdrive, causing stress.

Words like "too much work," "when, when, when," or "it is incomplete" trigger stress. The neurotransmitters in the brain immediately signal stress, triggering a cascade of chemical reactions throughout the body. If these chemicals do not get a proper outlet for release, they build up internally, manifesting as resentment and illness. This is why most people become so irritable under stress and resort to the only way they know to vent these chemicals: offloading their stress onto others.

If stress were confined to a single person, it would not be a cause for concern. However, it spreads from one person to another, then to a third, and so on, like a pandemic. Let's understand this vicious cycle of stress and how it ripples through our lives.

A person redirects their emotions, like anger, frustration, or stress, away from the actual source, onto another person or object that feels safer or more accessible. This is a subconscious way to avoid confronting the real source of stress, as that source may appear too powerful, unsafe, or inaccessible. It is a struggle between power and vulnerability. For example, if someone is upset with their boss but can't express it directly, they might come home and snap at a family member. While it may provide temporary relief, it can harm relationships and create cycles of negativity.

Often, offloading happens unknowingly. For example, a person consumed by their own thoughts trips over a stone and gets hurt. In anguish, they pick up the stone, mentally label it "stress," and hurl it at their neighbor's window. The neighbor, who is fast asleep, wakes up and feels stressed upon seeing their broken windowpane. They then frustratingly pick up shards of broken glass, label them "stress," and tuck them beneath their boss's seat.

In this way, everyone transfers their stress onto the other. Because people do not know the proper way to relieve their stress, they resort to offloading it onto others, mistakenly believing that giving it away will make them feel lighter.

To become stress-free, first stop the reflex to inflict your stress on others. Although offloading stress onto others offers a fleeting sense of relief, it sets off a chain reaction. The recipient of the stress will inevitably seek an outlet of their own, looking for another target. Eventually, that stress circles back to the original person, and this vicious cycle continues. It is crucial to stop this cycle.

To break free from this cycle, recognize your responsibility and take the initiative. Stop passing your stress on to others and calm yourself first. Let's understand this with a simple yet important meditation.

"My Self am present" meditation

Let us put whatever understanding we have gained so far into practice during this meditation, allowing it to sink deeply into our subconscious, so that all burdens of the mind dissolve at once.

First, read the instructions thoroughly before starting the meditation. While you can practice this meditation in your free time, it is most effective to practice it just before sleep. So, let's dive into this beautiful meditation.

1. Sit in a comfortable posture that makes your body feel relaxed.
2. Gently close your eyes and take a few deep breaths. Inhale deeply, then exhale slowly. Allow yourself to feel completely relaxed.
3. To begin, place your hand gently on your head with a sense of deep love and affection. Softly tell yourself, "You are my friend." Take a moment to allow the warmth of that connection to settle into your heart.

   Understand who you are referring to when you use the word "you." Just as we use "you" when speaking to another person, here you are addressing "you" to your body. This body is your friend; it helps you perform all your tasks. By referring to it as "you," you signal to your brain that you are distinct from your body, and you begin to feel a sense of detachment.
4. Command your brain, specifically the amygdala, to release all the stress stored in your memory. Place your hand on your head and say, "There is no emergency. No need for stress." Let go of the stress that is causing illness. Release it; it is no longer needed.

   Feel how your brain instantly obeys your command. Feel the changes happening in your body. Now, gently place your hands on your lap and fully experience this change.
5. In the second step, gently place your hand on your head once again, and affirm, "My Self am present." Feel it deeply

and say, "My Self am present" two to three times, letting the feeling sink in, i.e., "I am present."

The key is understanding who is being referred to as "My Self." It is the real you, the Self that you truly are. It is the sense of beingness that transcends the body, mind, and intellect. Feel that experience.

6. Realize that, in this very moment, you are present. The essence of who you truly are *is present.* Right now, you are in a state where you have to do nothing. There is a realization that you have never really done anything until now, and you are not going to do anything in the future either.

   All actions are being carried out by your friend, your body-mind mechanism. When there is nothing to do today and nothing to do in the future as well, feel a profound sense of relaxation that begins to emerge from this truth.

   By repeating "My Self am present," your brain is now completely relaxed because the Self is free from any stress of doing or not doing anything. Watch all actions unfold from this relaxed state, understanding that you are not the body, you are not the doer, you are free. Allow yourself to experience this sense of liberation.

7. You are with your body but liberated; you are in the present but free. Place your hand on your body, on your head, and affirm, "You are my friend." In that silent space, the truth becomes clear that you are separate from the body, and the body is your friend.

8. Offer love to this friend and say, "I like you. I love you. I respect you. It is because of you, my dear friend, that I have the opportunity to experience life and realize my own existence." Now, with this feeling of deep gratitude, bring your hand down.

9. Now, you simply *are.* You are free, you are the present.

With this feeling, a new way of thinking takes root in your body, and old, limiting beliefs begin to fade. This realization brings a new wave of energy and enthusiasm to your body. This enthusiasm will only grow as you dive deeper into the realization of "Who am I?" It is within this very human form that the realization of who you truly are happens.

10. Remain in this experience for a few moments, then slowly open your eyes. Notice how you feel.
11. Even after you finish the meditation, keep repeating the words "My Self am present" whenever you get the chance.

In this meditation, when you place your hand on your head and say "You are my friend" to your body, you are quietly declaring *I am not this body*. This simple acknowledgment is incredibly powerful, and repeating it brings significant transformation within. When we are unaware of the value of these practices, we usually drop them. But now, with the right understanding, we must begin to rewire the brain. Instead of following old patterns, we must initiate chemical changes in the brain in a new way so that it becomes an integral part of our life.

When a negative thought arises and causes pain, we instinctively identify with the body and declare, "I am troubled, I am sad, I am in pain." Without realizing it, this statement goes so deep that it makes sorrow and pain feel like an integral part of us. But the moment we say, "My Self am present," the Self, who we truly are, is revealed. It has always been there. We are simply awakening it by making this declaration, after which all the inner feelings transform instantly. So let us dive inward now, as there is no time for stress!

Action plan:

Practice "My Self am present meditation."

Appendix

The Consequences of Stress – a Survey

Stress primarily affects a person's mind before it shows up in other areas of life. For various reasons, many people experience stress deep down without even realizing it. If the cause of stress persists for a long time, its impact becomes visible not only to the person but also to those around them.

When stress is not managed properly or addressed on time, it begins to affect the body, eventually manifesting as health issues. The consequences of stress extend across all aspects of life, including physical, mental, financial, social, and spiritual well-being. Let's explore its effects one by one.

1. Physical plane

The numerous stresses encountered in life can adversely affect various organs of the body, including the brain, lungs, heart, blood vessels, kidneys, intestines, and muscles. Stress influences all parts of the circulatory system, including the heart and its arteries. Prolonged stress increases blood pressure, placing extra strain on the heart and increasing the risk of cardiac ailments. Prolonged stress also affects the functioning of the digestive and respiratory systems.

The worst effect of excessive stress is on the immune system—the body's protective shield. When bacteria or viruses attack the body, the immune system fights them off, preventing disease. However, stress weakens this defense system, leaving the body vulnerable to illness.

A person who is constantly under stress often becomes addicted to alcohol, smoking, or other substances. Although these addictions might provide temporary relief from stress, they are extremely harmful to one's health in the long run. Ultimately, one harms oneself both physically and mentally.

2. Mental plane

Stress has severe effects on one's mental health. When one fails to cope with daily stress, they fall into deep despair, anxiety, and depression. Feelings of apathy, hopelessness, and agitation, often expressed as anger, dominate their life. Their existence becomes aimless, and the very desire to attain joy, fulfillment, and success fades away.

Nature has designed a mechanism that prevents humans from enduring excessive pressure. For example, when someone experiences unbearable pain, they become unconscious. Similarly, when stress becomes overwhelming, one may lose the ability to cope and suffer a mental breakdown, eventually leading to insanity.

3. Financial plane

One major cause of stress is financial instability and unpredictability. Often, people spend money just because of societal pressure or to keep up with others—be it for festivals, birthday parties, vacations, or recreational activities. They fulfill all their children's demands, buying expensive mobile phones, laptops, and cars, believing these to be necessities of modern life. To afford these, they sometimes have to take loans, but they hesitate to discuss their financial situation openly with their family. This results in financial stress.

When this financial stress intensifies, it begins to affect their work performance. Their work efficiency declines, and the likelihood of mistakes increases. As a result, they cannot advance in their careers, further worsening their financial condition. In some cases, they may even lose their job, leading to even greater stress.

4. Social plane

When there is a family conflict at home, it is natural for someone to vent their frustration at work. This can lead to strained relationships with colleagues, reduced teamwork, and a sense of isolation. Conversely, if someone faces workplace conflicts or pressure, they may vent their frustration on family members, leading to bitterness in personal relationships. Over time, this cycle of stress can damage both personal and professional interactions, making it difficult to maintain a balanced, healthy social life.

5. Spiritual plane

Many people believe in some form of God and have faith that a higher power is always with them, guiding and protecting them. However, when overwhelmed by stress, negativity begins to grow within them. They fail to see any solutions to their problems, which weakens their faith and patience. In such situations, some people may even lean toward atheism, questioning, "If God really exists, I would not be in this situation; my problems would have been solved."

As they fail to perceive stress correctly, they are unable to understand the lessons life is trying to teach them. Challenges are meant for personal growth, not to cause distress. By solving one problem, they move to the next level of growth, where even bigger challenges arise to push them further along the path of development. If they reflect on their past problems, they will realize that every challenge has ultimately contributed to their growth. However, this realization is only possible when they maintain a positive outlook, have faith, and remain patient.

Survey report

Considering the various negative impacts of stress, several surveys have been conducted to help people understand the importance of leading a stress-free life. Some survey reports are presented below for reference.

Global Stress Statistics

According to the Gallup State of the Global Workplace: 2026 Report and the WHO Health at a Glance 2025, the world remains at a historical high for emotional distress.

1. **Daily Stress Prevalence:** 40% of employees worldwide reported experiencing significant stress "a lot of the previous day."
2. **Demographic Peaks:**
    - **Age:** Stress is highest among midlife adults (ages 30–49), who also report the lowest sleep quality.
    - **Work Style:** Hybrid and on-site remote-capable workers report the highest stress (46%), compared to exclusively remote workers (41%).
3. **Economic Impact:** Stress-related anxiety and depression cost the global economy approximately $1 trillion per year in lost productivity.
4. **Most Stressed Regions:** North America (United States and Canada) currently leads the world with 50% of the workforce reporting daily stress.

India Stress Statistics

Reports from the PIB (Ministry of Health) and recent 2025–2026 observational studies highlight a significant "treatment gap" and rising urban pressures.

1. **General Prevalence:** Roughly 11% of Indian adults live with a diagnosable mental health disorder, with stress being the primary underlying trigger.

2. **Stress Severity:** In recent surveys of Indian adults:
    - 84.9% report experiencing moderate stress.
    - 5.5% report severe stress.
3. **The Gender Gap:** Women in India report significantly higher stress levels than men. Nearly 20% of Indian women experience anxiety or depression, compared to 10% of men.
4. **The Treatment Gap:** A staggering 70% to 92% of Indians suffering from stress-related disorders do not receive proper treatment due to social stigma or lack of access to professionals.
5. **Primary Stressors in India:**
    - **Academic/Job Pressure:** Cited by over 36% of younger adults.
    - **Financial Problems:** Cited by 20.7% of the population.
6. **Urban vs. Rural:** Stress and mental health disorders are nearly twice as prevalent in urban areas (13.5%) compared to rural areas (6.9%), largely due to digital overload and environmental factors like pollution.

Summary Comparison Table

Feature	**Global Average**	**India**
High/Extreme pressure	91%	~85%
Daily stress rate	37%	~53% (Urban areas)
Primary risk group	18-24 (Gen Z)	Under 35
Primary stressor	Inflation/work	Academic/job, financial

You can mail your opinion or feedback on this book to: books.feedback@tejgyan.org

About Sirshree

Sirshree's spiritual quest, which began during his childhood, led him on a journey through various schools of philosophy and meditation practices. He studied a wide range of literature on mind science and spirituality. After a long period of deep contemplation on the truth of life, his quest culminated in attaining the ultimate truth.

Sirshree espouses, "All spiritual paths that lead to the truth begin differently but culminate at the same point – Understanding. This understanding is complete in itself. Listening to this understanding is enough to attain the Truth." Over the last two decades, he has dedicated his life to raise mass consciousness.

Sirshree has delivered more than 4000 discourses that throw light on this understanding. He has designed a system for wisdom, which makes it accessible to all. This system has inspired people from all walks of life to progress on their journey of the Truth. Thousands of seekers join in a virtual prayer for World Peace and Global Healing daily at 9:09 am and 9:09 pm.

About Tej Gyan Foundation

Tej Gyan Foundation is a non-profit organization founded on the teachings of Sirshree. The Foundation disseminates Tejgyan – the wisdom that guides one from self-development to Self-realization, leading towards Self-stabilization.

The Foundation's system for imparting wisdom has been assessed by international quality auditors and accredited with the ISO 9001:2015 certification. This wisdom has been presented in a simple, systematic, and practically applicable form that makes it accessible to people from all walks of life, regardless of religion, caste, social strata, country, or belief system.

The Foundation has centers in more than 400 cities and towns across India and other countries. The mission of Tej Gyan Foundation is to create a highly evolved society by leading seekers from negative thoughts to positive thoughts and further, from positive thoughts to Happy thoughts. A 'Happy thought' is the auspicious thought of being free from all thoughts, leading to the state of supreme bliss beyond thoughts.

If you seek such wisdom that leads you beyond mere knowledge, dissolves all problems, frees you from all limiting beliefs, reveals the true nature of divinity, and establishes you in the ultimate truth, then it is time to discover Tejgyan; it is time to rise above the mundane knowledge of words and experience Tejgyan!

The MahaAasmani Magic of Awakening Retreat

Self-development to Self-realization towards Self-stabilization

Do you wish to experience unconditional happiness that is not dependent on any reason? Happiness that is permanent and only increases with time? Do you wish to experience love, peace, self-belief, harmony in relationships, prosperity, and true contentment? Do you wish to progress in all facets of your life, viz. physical, mental, social, financial, and spiritual?

If you seek answers to these questions and are thirsty for the ultimate truth, then you are welcome to participate in the MahaAasmani Magic of Awakening retreat organized by Tej Gyan Foundation. This is the Foundation's flagship retreat based on the teachings of Sirshree.

The purpose of this retreat

The purpose of this retreat is that every human being should:

- Discover the answer to "Who am I" and "Why am I?" through direct experience and be established in ultimate bliss.
- Learn the art of living in the present, free from the burden of the past and the anxiety of the future.
- Acquire practical tools to help quieten the chattering mind and dissolve problems.
- Discover missing links in the practices of Meditation (*Dhyana*), Action (*Karma*), Wisdom (*Gyana*), and Devotion (*Bhakti*).

Tej Gyan Foundation – Contact details

Registered Office:
Happy Thoughts Building, Vikrant Complex, Near Tapovan Mandir, Pimpri, Pune 411017, INDIA. Contact: +91 20-27411240, +91 20-27412576

MaNaN Ashram:
Survey No. 43, Sanas Nagar, Nandoshi Gaon, Kirkatwadi Phata, Off Sinhagad Road, Taluka Haveli, Pune district - 411024, INDIA. Contact: +91 992100 8060.

WORLD PEACE PRAYER

Divine Light of Love, Bliss, and Peace is Showering;
The Golden Light of Higher Consciousness is Rising;
All negativity on Earth is Dissolving;
Everyone is in Peace and Blissfully Shining;
O God, Gratitude for Everything!

Members of Tej Gyan Foundation have been offering this impersonal mass prayer for many years. Those who are happy can offer this prayer. Those feeling low or suffering from illness can receive healing with this prayer.

If you are feeling troubled or sick, please sit to receive the healing effect of this prayer. Visualize that the divine white healing light is being showered on earth through the prayers of thousands and is also reaching you, bringing you peace and good health. You can dwell in this feeling for some time and then offer your gratitude to those offering the prayer.

A Humble Appeal

More than a million peace lovers pray for World Peace and Global Healing every morning and evening at 9:09. Also, a prayer (in Hindi) to elevate consciousness is webcast every day on YouTube at 3:30 pm and 9:00 pm IST. Please participate in this noble endeavor.

www.ingramcontent.com/pod-product-compliance
Lightning Source LLC
Chambersburg PA
CBHW031350230926
51848CB00002B/466